GOD TAKE OVER

God, Take Over;
I Am Finished

A Cry for Mercy When Suffering Seems Unfair

Catherine Agada

Unless otherwise indicated, Scriptures verses used in this book are taken from The Holy Bible, *New International Version®, NIV® Copyright © 1973, 1978, 1984, 2011 by Biblica, Inc.® Used by permission. All rights reserved worldwide. And from King James (KJ) version. Public Domain Or from Good News Holy Bible (GN) Public Domain.*

"Jesus Messages" are taken from The Book of Truth by Coma Books *Copyright © Maria Divine Mercy, 2012.* www.thewarningsecondcooming.com/messages/all-messages *Used by permission. All rights reserved.*

Inspiration for Daily Living modified from the author's original title: "Making It Work: Inspirations for Christian Marriage and Life" by Catherine Aniebonam (Agada) 2006.

Book Cover Design and image by HappyDesigner

GOD, TAKE OVER; I AM FINISHED

Copyright © 2013 Catherine Ngozi Agada

Published by CTK Publishing
Dallas, Texas
www.ctkpublishing.net

ISBN:0615810438
ISBN-13:9780615810430

Printed in the United State of America by CreateSpace

DEDICATION

This book is dedicated to the Mother of God, Mother of Salvation, Paragon of Humility, and Exemplar of All God's Children. Mother Mary, we love you.

For he has been mindful of the humble state of his servant.
From now on all generations will call me blessed. (Luke 1:48 NIV)

You are not alone!

For every bad situation or challenge you are going through,

know that someone else has gone through that and survived,

or is currently going through it somewhere and will survive.

And so will YOU!

Cathy Ngozi Agada
Daughter of the King

CONTENTS

INSPIRATIONS FOR DAILY LIVING

PRAYERS

ACKNOWLEDGMENTS

All glory, thanks, honor, and adoration belong to my God the Father of all mankind and to His son Jesus Christ who made us free, and the Holy Spirit, who inspires every good work.

I would like to acknowledge and thank my dearest mother, (Chief) Mrs. Catherine Agada, my greatest inspiration, who is always there for her family. And to my siblings, I am grateful to God to have a family of prayer warriors: Sis Emily, Rose, Simon, Stella, Sylvia, Ifeoma, and Ebele, I love you and the entire family.

I also acknowledge in a very special way all my dear friends, business and prayer partners whose names cannot fit in here. To all of you, I say thank you. To Dr. JC Aniagolu-Johnson, I thank you for allowing the Holy Spirit to use you to minister to me, and to Uju Odobulu, my sister and friend, thanks for being part of my editing team.

Finally, to the visionary Maria Divine Mercy and the entire JTM/MDM group, I thank you for selflessly doing the Master's work, and for granting me permission to share our Lord's messages with a disbelieving and hurting world.

PREFACE

As I thought about an intriguing preface for this book, I came across some "messages" from our Lord Jesus Christ that were given to a European visionary and prophet, Maria Divine Mercy, published in *The Book of Truth* by Coma Books,[i] and referenced by permission from thewarningsecondcoming.com. These messages are to be shared as part of the urgent call for evangelism to prepare mankind for the Second Coming of Christ. I realized that the message dated April 25, 2011, titled "All Mankind Will Have Free Will until Their Will Unites with the Divine Will of the Father," and a few others summarized and explained some of the experiences I was writing about, as well as some lessons I am trying to convey in this book.

The experiences I share in *God, Take Over; I Am Finished* reveal how God manifests Himself in special ways to us during crisis and in weakness when we surrender our self-will to His divine will. As I share part of this message that touched my heart, I pray that you too will open your heart to what you may discover.

According to the message "All Mankind Will Have Free Will until Their Will Unites with the Divine Will of the Father," Jesus laments that many souls do not acknowledge Him simply because they don't want to, even though they know Him. The message said:

It is only when people are afflicted by tragedy that they stop and think of death and any future life they believe may be ahead. This is why I sometimes punish those souls, out of My Mercy, to bring them to their senses so I can save them. Through suffering, all those material attractions, sought out by the senses, will become meaningless and be seen for what they are—fleeting novelties which will vanish within a short period of time.[ii]

The messages and prayers to Maria Divine Mercy (MDM) started in 2010. Maria said she was told the messages were to be published *exactly* as she received them - with no changes whatsoever to the contents. She accepts that divine revelations are not necessary to one's belief in God. According to Maria, the messages' purposes are to help improve people's faith and help prepare them for events in the world that relate to the period of time preceding the Second Coming of Christ.

God, Take Over; I Am Finished is a cry for the mercy of God when the cross you bear seems too heavy and the surrender of self-will at the realization that if God doesn't help you, no one else can. I pray again that you will receive the divine revelations, allow them to speak directly to your heart, and discern His messages not logically, but from the peace, discomfort, or tears that may come from within.

INTRODUCTION

The best teacher, they say, is experience. As I reminisced on the good life received, the pains and hardship I had endured, the trials and tribulations I had overcome, and the struggles that I faced every day to be free, I realized that I had enough to pour out to fill a book, all to the glory of God. *God, Take Over; I Am Finished* came out of personal experiences and testimonies, inspirations from the Holy Spirit, divine knowledge and the Word of God, as a result of my willingness and sometimes unwillingness to submit and surrender to God's leading.

I am very elated as well as frightened to pour out my soul in this book to you, my readers. At the same time, I am humbled as a vessel through which God may speak to you directly or indirectly through the experiences, testimonies, divine words, and messages shared in this book. So, be prepared; I suggest grabbing a box of tissues in case you decide to weep for me or for yourself at the realization that you are not alone in your struggles. Those who knew me before now may be surprised, yet not perplexed, for the signs were there all along as soon as the hand of God took hold of me, despite my resistance to His total submission.

God, Take Over; I Am Finished started as a story about my wilderness experience and my journey through the afflictions and trials allowed by God to humble, purify, rewire, and reposition me to be worthy to be used by Him. As I started writing, however, the Spirit of the Lord had more for me to say, and so I found myself bringing awareness to God's end-time messages (revealed in *The Book of Truth*) in answer to His call to evangelize and pray for humanity. In addition, I felt an urge to republish the daily living inspirations that were part of my book, *Making It Work*, written in 2006 (published by iUniverse). The inspirations for daily living are to be used as a faith-building guide to help you *love better, live happier, pray better, and forgive faster to enjoy the fullness of the life Christ offers us.*

There are two ways readers can approach this book. One way is from the standpoint of one who is tired of running, hiding, or doing it your way, and now ready to try God's way, after realizing your human limitations, inabilities, weaknesses, or failures; you are ready to submit and hand it over because, frankly, you have no other choice at this point. Or it could be approached with the attitude of one who is ready to give-in or give-up because things have not worked out as expected, despite much praying and doing your best to follow God. You cry out for mercy because you are tired, upset or, frustrated.

Both approaches will lead to the same realization that where weakness abides, grace prevails; where human strength ends, God's begins; and when human senses, will-power, intelligence, ability, and knowledge fail, God's supremacy manifests. Reading this book brings healing to the soul, inspires a childlike faith, and restores love and hope in God.

Finally, God Take Over; I Am Finished is also for anyone on a spiritual cross-road who has a yearning for more of God and could use a spiritual boost, including those who seek to discover the God they already know—the I AM, Who-Is, Who-Was, and Who-Is-To-Come.

GOD, WHERE ARE YOU?

Happy is the man whom God chastises! Do not reject the punishment of the almighty. For he wounds, but he binds up; he smites, but his hands give healing...

(Job 5, 17-18)

I still remember kneeling down in front of my living room alter one afternoon, asking God, "What's going on? I mean, what is really happening to me, God? Are You still there? How come You have not been hearing me—or have You? How come I have been praying and begging You to improve this particular situation in my home for over two years, but instead of helping, You let it get worse? What's up with that, Lord? What have I not done? Tell me what I have done wrong."

As the questions poured from my mouth, I felt hot tears running down from my eyes and pain in my chest like it would explode. I could not comprehend what I was hearing or believe what I was seeing; I was not prepared for what I was about to go through.

Up until 2008, I'd always had it good and considered myself blessed and lucky to be given so much. I already knew that everything I had come from God and by His grace. Before then, I used to think that I was just smart and hardworking. But, you see, you are only successful to the extent of the strength of God poured in you and the unmerited favors and grace bestowed on you by the Creator, who gives freely to all His children (both the good and the bad) as He chooses.

Still kneeling in His presence, I let out a loud sob as I saw everything going down. First it was my marriage, next my job and finances; and, as if that was not enough, my health also. The attack was so fierce and unrelenting that I thought God either wanted to kill me or absolutely didn't want to be bothered right now. I remembered wondering throughout my ordeal whether God realized I was only one person to face so much at the same time: really, seriously, just one person, Lord! Yet His word kept flashing to console me as He whispered, "My grace is sufficient for you [my child], for My power is made perfect in weakness" (2 Cor. 12:9).

My marriage had just crashed, and I could not understand exactly what happened. Imagine living with a man and receiving a call from an outsider letting you know that your husband is leaving you. Imagine a different person calling to find out what's going on because your husband just ordered your home to be listed on the market and you— clue-l-e-s-s. I remembered going through my mind trying to recollect what I might have done wrong. How may I have upset him, I kept asking myself? I'm not sure. I kept pondering on the last conversation we had before he stopped talking to me. Could it be because I asked that he join me in praying with blessed oil? No, maybe not! Could be because I asked him for a little support on expenses I thought to myself, I don't know. But all I can remember was that we didn't have a quarrel that could have led to this. Confused and dismayed, I went straight to my praying alter to let it out and to find out why I set myself up and God did not try to stop me.

Funny, how I went from questioning to realization that I, not God, made the mess. I chose my ex, not God, because I was not patient enough to wait for my own Boaz, or to heed the warning signs. How many of you know what I am talking about right now? I was still crying and crying. To be honest, I was not crying for the loss of the man, but for the many prayers, efforts, and much more invested in the marriage that had gone down the drain. I was crying because I was also worried about what people would say: "God, You know I am innocent!" I cried out with a heavy heart. "Why, Lord, why me again?" I sobbed.

For a moment my mind fleshed back to the pains of my earlier marriage. We were young and he is not a bad guy, but his love for alcohol cost him a lot including his marriage. My poor ex would go straight from work to the bar (beer parlor as it was called), and would come home way late into the night and used me as a punching bag. Sadly enough his addiction and extreme insecurity drove me to flee for safety leaving everything behind and never looked back.

This time what were the issues or my crime? I don't know. But I realized that because I had decided to accept the call of God to serve Him, I became a target for the evil one. In obedience to the Holy Spirit, I started a ministry and gathered some beautiful sisters (DOK) together so we could stand up for God through worship gatherings. I never knew that in so doing, I disrupted the kingdom of darkness, and so an "arrest warrant" was out on me, and an attack unleashed for me to be disgraced and destroyed by evil forces. Indeed, it all started going down after that.

In the midst of the marriage drama, I lost my high-paying job. But that was just icing on the cake, because I still had a business to fall back on; thank God for that. Yet it was bad timing to be out of a steady income, being all alone. I took solace in the fact that God had just blessed me with a new business opportunity. But what do you know? Not long after I had invested and finished setting up the business, I received the dreadful news that all of my investment was in jeopardy. Some imported merchandise that I was expecting to arrive on time for a client was seized by US Customs for some crazy reason and all marked to be shipped back.

Talk about "when it rains, it pours!" I thought about my client and my investment and knew that if that happens, it would be very devastating. This was all I could take at that point, so I went back to my altar to settle some scores with God. I felt cornered in a box and knew that if God didn't help me, I would be finished. "God, God, where are You? Please don't let this happen to me," I wept bitterly.

The battle was on, so I went full force into prayer, and you know what? God will never lead you to where His grace cannot support you, no matter the storm. He will not allow you to be tried beyond your limits. This is why Proverbs 3:5 advises us to lean not on our own understanding in all we do, but submit and trust in the Lord. Jesus offered us His yoke to make our burdens light, unlike the yoke of the devil (Matt. 11:30).

Eventually, customs released the goods, and the show was able to go on. I thought it was over, but it had only just begun. The Lord allowed me to go through the wilderness experience for a purpose. I cannot even begin to describe my experiences in the few years that followed. Numerous attempts were made on my life, but God canceled all contracts of death and declared that I "will not die but live to proclaim what He, the LORD has done" (Psa. 118:17).

How do I know that there was a contract on my life by the evil ones? Because I know that everything happens first in the spiritual realm before it manifests in the physical. If you are privileged to know, God can show it to you before it happens in dreams, or reveal it by prophecy as a warning, or as His way to let you know the battle fought and won in your favor. The attacks on my life to take me out were unquestionable. God constantly showed them to me in dreams and revealed some of them in prophecy. "The kings of the earth rise up and the princes conspire together against the Lord and against His Anointed. From his throne in heaven the Lord laughs and mocks their feeble plans" (Psa. 2:2, 4).

In the dreams, I often saw myself standing by the roadside watching as my car got totaled in severe accidents and towed away. In one dream, a big sea mammal (fur seal or leviathan I think) swallowed me up and spit me out again (I was too hot for it), like Jonah in the Bible, except that the animal was bigger than a whale, and this happened in an open field, not in the water. Before it came, I saw a swarm of bees released on me in that same field, but they did not touch me because of God's covering over my life. That same night, I saw a helicopter hovering around me with the largest and longest metal chain I'd ever seen, trying to chain me to the spot where I was sitting, but the heavy metal narrowly missed me.

The grand finale came in another dream: after all the other disguised attempts failed, the demon himself appeared to suffocate me in my hospital bed three times. Each time, I screamed the name of Jesus, and after the last attempt, he released his hold on me, looked at me hatefully, and left. That was the last time I saw his ugly behind. Two of the accidents occurred later in the physical, but I was unharmed each time; only my car was totaled, like I saw it in the dream.

Why am I telling you all these stories? Because I went through some stuff that are not ordinary; and some of you who might be experiencing similar or facing other difficult situations might be encouraged and strengthened. I want you to know that if God is for you, no one can be against you and succeed, and if God does not approve it, no one can take your life. My mom is another living example of when God says no, because He holds the keys to our lives.

"Who is he that said, and it comes to pass, when the Lord commands it not?" (Lam. 3:37).

But you must be able to protect yourself with prayers, and have faith in God's power to save, heal, and provide for you and your family; otherwise, you leave the door wide open for the enemy to come in and steal from you. Without faith, the enemy disarms you by paralyzing you with fear, doubt, worry, anxiety, distractions, and weakness in prayer. Or, worse still, he sneaks up on you with self-condemnation, using your weakness and the state of mind and heart that is soiled with un-forgiveness, bitterness, anger, resentment, jealousy, etc. to hinder your prayers.

Please understand that I am only giving my testimony here to glorify God. It is the least of the witnessing I have been called to do in order to testify to God's power and glory before a disbelieving and hurting world. By the way, self-condemnation is one of the devil's tools to make you believe that God's mercy is limited and deters you from going to the throne of mercy to receive grace and help for your need and struggles. Fortunately, that's his lie and not the truth. The truth is that God's mercy endures forever (Ps. 136:1), and His love and faithfulness continues through all generations (Ps. 100:5).

To continue my ordeal, another attack came; this time, the evil one launched a fierce and incessant attack on my finances. Did he really attack my money? "Yes" is an understatement. To give you a picture of what was going on, there were periods when I would not receive a single call for business (even though my business line had previously never stopped ringing). If I manage to make a sale, the client would come back for a refund right after; and some would return to complain seriously with no justification. It was a trial period, and because I live on business income alone, I relied on amazing grace for providence. Very strange things were happening, because the enemy knew that once my finances were weakened, I would be broken. But I was undaunted, and having done everything in obedience, I remained standing! "For the Lord is my shepherd; I have everything I need" (Psa. 23:1). Above all, because I knew what was going on and understood that the weapon of my warfare was not carnal (2 Cor. 10:4); I fought back with faith and prayer power.

Nevertheless, I was finally broken when my health came under attack in the midst of all the other struggles. Talk about life being unfair. Let me tell you, there are three areas that the devil targets to destroy believers so that we will either defame God or lose faith and backslide. The three are: marriage, health, and finance. If not for my prayer-warrior family, my angelic intercessors and prayer partners that God planted to hold me up (God bless each and every one of you), I would have been inconsolable. Yet on the outside, you will never know the battle inside. Even my sweet sisters didn't know half of my ordeal as close as we are, bless their hearts.

Finally, I was no longer in control and had to surrender all to Him: "I am finished; God, take over."

OKAY GOD, I AM FINISHED; TAKE OVER

*Their purpose is to prove that your faith is genuine. Even gold, which can
be destroyed, is tested by fire; and so your faith, which is much more precious
than gold, must also be tested, Then you will receive praise and glory and
honor on the Day when Jesus Christ is revealed.*

(1 Peter 1:7)

I remember one day lying on my bed crying with the Bible open and
reading Psalms, from Psalm 1 to the end. The idea was to read the
entire book of Psalms that day, lest the one psalm needed for my
situation be left out. I wanted to leverage with God that day for His
mercy. As they say, desperate situations call for desperate measures. It
seems funny now, but not so funny then.

As I read, the tears kept rolling and soaking my pillow. I was
crying because I was weak, tired, and helpless. I am not talking about
just physical or emotional tiredness: I mean complete and extreme
fatigue that would overpower my entire body such that I could not
function properly even after I woke up from sleep. Of course, the
emotional weakness (stress factor) was also there, but less damaging,
because my spirit was never completely broken. I still had a glimpse of
hope that this, too, would pass. Yet the physical body was no longer in
alignment with my equilibrium.

I held on to God's reassuring words and promises that; "many
are the afflictions of the righteous but the Lord delivers him from them
all" (Psa. 34:19). I understood by faith that we are not to look at the

troubles we see now; rather, to fix our eyes on things that cannot yet be seen (which we believe), for the things we see now will pass away and the things we cannot see now will last forever (2 Cor. 4:18). As God began to separate me from certain attachments, I surrounded myself with spiritual support system—prayer partners, fellowship, and family night vigils. I made adoration of the Blessed Sacrament[iii] a priority where I go to receive divine visitation, peace, and strength when my body, mind, and spirit are weak.

When you go through unexplainable events and trials more powerful than you are, my advice is to *never* isolate yourself in secrecy. Instead, surround yourself with a strong prayer group or partner to pray with you and for you. You need someone you can talk to who understands spiritual matters and can minister the divine Word of God to encourage and motivate you. But please be careful of where you go for help; this is not a time to go to a fake prophet or church where you will be manipulated to give up money, lied to about the source of your problem, and turned against your family for someone else's selfish glory and gain.

The truth is that what you go through in life may not be about what you did or didn't do, or who is after you. Sometimes it's about how much God wants to get your attention for a higher calling, to move you to a different level, or to save your soul. No one can understand the mind of God, yet His ways and wisdom can be found during trials and hardships by those who are patient enough to go through what it takes to mature.

I finally came to rest and rely not on my own strength and power, but on God alone. I gingered myself up with the Word of God, cast all my burdens on Him, and allowed His joy to become my strength. It would have done me no good to soak in a pity party; that was what the enemy wanted in the first place, to see me miserable. When you are accustomed to running to the Lord on your knees in truth and in spirit, and to praising Him no matter the circumstance, He gives you His supernatural strength to sustain you, His wisdom to guide you, and His favor to open doors of breakthrough that no man can shut. Amen!

Make no mistake, God did not cause me this pain; He allowed it for a purpose, but His grace was sufficient to see me through it. He got my attention, all right, and I learned to become a worshiper. Let me tell you, when you go through the dry valley or wilderness experience like I did, spiritual warfare will not get you out of it quickly. Seed-sowing (giving) can help, but will not deliver you from the purification by the hand of God, although your seed will be recorded in heaven for the harvest time. It is only going into His presence and meeting one-on-one with Him in worship, praise, and adoration despite your own pains that quickly opens heaven and causes the mighty hand of God to extend and lift you out of darkness.

Believe me; you will know when you've arrived, because during worship, His divine love envelops and comforts you with strength, as divine hope pulls you out of despair. You suddenly become certain that "this, too, shall pass," according to His promises. You may still be hurting and crying, but you are praising God; you are still suffering, but you are thanking God because you have hope for tomorrow. If you can relate to that, shout, "Alleluia!"

Anyhow, going back to my story, I went full force into serving God. And after a while, everything went back to normal for me, and I started receiving favors again in my business. God allowed me extra favors and helped me flourish even more. I thought I was good with God by then, yet I struggled with total submission and became extremely distracted again as I joined the rat race, chasing after material things to meet my expectations.

Remember, serving God and surrendering to Him are two different things. I started walking ahead of God and went back to my old self-willed attitude, especially in the area of personal and business decisions. God has a sense of humor and it goes like this: "If you don't ask or seek My opinion before you make your decision(s), when it crashes on your face, deal with it and leave Me out of it until you are ready to admit, submit, and release it to My control with no interference."

Let me tell you a story of how walking ahead of God almost cost me my life. God warned me in a dream about what would happen, but I did not understand the impact of that dream. I knew it was a bad dream and canceled it at once when I woke up, but unfortunately I did not realize that more prayer and fasting were required to mitigate its impact and or stop it from manifesting. In the dream, I saw myself wearing a shabby cloth, looking dejected. I could not walk straight without wobbling or falling down. I entered an arena filled with people in ceremonial dress, but there was no one willing to lend me support as I wobbled. Finally, I saw myself in another part of the arena, and my younger sister saw me and took me into the powder room to clean me up. "Look at you; Ngozi, she called me by my native name (meaning "Blessing"), see where you have ended up," she said to me as she helped.

Not long after I had the dream, it came to pass, and if not for God's mercy that mitigated my suffering, I would have died in Nigeria. What happened was that I had flown down to Nigeria for business even though I had all the signs not to travel then. Two days after getting into the country, I began to feel weak and tired. I asked a friend for her doctor's name, and my cousin took me to the clinic. Immediately after I got there, I was admitted. My sugar level was off the chart. Within a twinkle of two days, I had lost so much weight and become so weak and pitiful that I could barely walk straight without wobbling. I didn't want to alarm my family, so I did not call them immediately, since a doctor friend of mine was there.

To relate that experience to what I saw in my dream, I wobbled in the physical because my legs were unable to bear my new weight, especially when climbing the stairs; that was how bad it was. Remarkably, that same sister I saw in the dream was the one who came to my side in Nigeria. Worried as she was, she flew down to encourage me and offered advice on where she saw missteps on my part. That was why she was the one in my dream cleaning me up.

Even though I spoke to God on a daily basis and God had tried to warn me, I was too anxious to move ahead, and nearly paid the price with my life. In fairness to myself, I did take it to God in prayer over again, but I guess I was blinded by my own eagerness to move forward at that time and failed to discern God's silence. I made some poor decisions, not only on the timing, but especially on some partnership ventures. I knew God had spoken concerning my prosperity, yet I moved sooner than His leading. Usually, God's silence on a matter means to wait and keep praying about it until you feel a release in your spirit and, it could come with a sign of confirmation.

So, the first lesson for you, my readers, is that God will always show up ahead of time and warn you about potential dangers (whether it is through intuition, a dream, restlessness and not having peace about a person, situation, or action, etc.) when you are still and not too distracted to hear. The second lesson is that trusting in God without surrendering to his leading is ineffective. I had prayed seriously, but if

I'd waited for confirmation, maybe the timing for that particular trip would have been different, including not melding into that business relationship in the first place.

This experience and a few others finally led me to the place of submission and surrender of self-will. I knew beyond a doubt that if I didn't allow God to lead, I would never achieve my full potential even if I managed to make it big. Therefore, "Lord, take over—Your will, Your way" has been my prayer and attitude ever since! I tried it my way, I resisted and I suffered as a result. Even though the suffering seemed unfair at times, yet, the lessons learned and the victory achieved as a result made meaning out of the suffering.

In everything therefore, give God the glory. In every trial or tribulation, there is a lesson and an opportunity to turn it around for good if you allow His will, His way and His time. For we know, according to Romans 8:28, that all things work together for good to them that love God, to them who are the called according to his purpose." I realized that the period of my dry and wilderness experience was not all in vain. For in the pain, I gained the following graces:

1. **Dependency on God Alone** -- I learn to lean on God alone; going from self-sufficiency to dependency on God.
2. **Preparedness** – A period of separation from the crowd and deeper relationship with God. I focused on God; praying more, reading His word and inspirational materials and engaging in spiritual exercises to get myself ready for the tasks and ministry that God wants to place in my path.
3. **Reprioritization** – I was forced to give up excessive quest for materialism and to spend more time in His presence. I learned to be a worshiper.

4. **Hearing from God** – It became an opportunity to learn to listen and hear when God speaks, and to communicate in Spirit.

5. **Attitude Change** – I experienced what it is to "have" and to "have not", and now live in gratitude for everything I have. I understood that promotion comes only from God—it is never by human might. I also have a much better appreciation and respect for the less privileged!

Relax, "I Am" Still in Control

When you pass through the waters, I will be with you;
and when you pass through the rivers, they will not sweep over you.
When you walk through the fire, you will not be burned;
the flames will not set you ablaze....

(Isa. 43:2)

Every experience in life is for a purpose. Every lesson learned as a result is for teaching and for building up of yourself and others. It did not take me long to realize why I had to pass through the hand of God's purification; if only one person is helped or encouraged by this book, God is already glorified.

We know that God has called each and every one of us for a purpose and allowed mankind to freely choose to answer or not. However, when some kind of traumatic experience comes knocking, whether because of your own mistakes or because of an attack from enemies or evil forces, there is a purpose. Purification and discipline come in these crises to shape us. Often the suffering seems unfair, even unjust, to our human reasoning. Yet God is with us during the ordeal and in tune with our everyday issues, big and small. The purification could be intended to redirect your attention to the purpose of your calling, to wake you up to your full potential, and ultimately to draw you nearer to Him.

Have you ever found yourself in a situation where you plea-bargained with God in desperation: "Lord, if You do a, b, c, I will not do x, y, z?" Have you ever been angry at God enough for something He did or didn't do and decided to take matters into your own hands? You went off on your own and did what you had to do in your own way, before realizing that your way was not working either, and then cried out to the Lord for divine intervention.

What about despairing to the point of giving up on a particular situation that you prayed about for years, especially if you did all you could and God remained silent? In frustration, you may have lamented, "You know, God, I have done everything You required me to do. I have listened to Your Word, prayed, fasted, given to charity, and tithed, but You don't seem to be listening. I don't know what else to do." In your heart, you may have murmured, "Lord, why do You hate me and why are You punishing me? I have served You well, yet You seem to have abandoned me." Finally, when you'd had enough, you cried out, "Lord, take over; I am finished!"

If you can relate to any of the scenarios described above, know that you are not alone. Many people are in this boat, but the "I AM" is still in control. Perhaps you have taken it to Him in prayer before. Don't be discouraged; God is still able to destroy every yoke of sin and sorrow off your shoulders. He has been waiting on you to surrender and let Him take over. He wishes to lead you, heal you, fight your battles, renew you, and bless you. It may seem impossible now, but God can do all things with your permission.

The truth is that, just as God cannot force His will on mankind, He will not force His divine intervention on you without your invitation and cooperation, initiated in prayer and accepted by faith. You must believe without a doubt that God can do what He said He would do, and can change any situation you have. Remember, God's denial could be a blessing in disguise. If you haven't taken it to God in prayer before now, start today. And if you have, but your actions indicate you have not yet released control of the situation to Him due to fear, worry, anxiousness or doubt, you need to repent and ask for forgiveness. Fear, which leads to doubt is the devil's tool to undermine God's power and deny us our blessings. The Scripture is clear in James 1-7 that no double-minded man can expect to receive anything from the Lord.

Prayer is the key and the weapon of our warfare; faith is our shield and defiance; but love conquers it all. You may have been distracted and taken your eyes off God for a while, and all of a sudden God may seem very far away. Relax and look around you—God could not have been nearer to you! God never abandons His own. He is waiting to be allowed into the sanctuary of your heart. Because of man's free will, you must choose to seek God to find that He is near.

For Catholics (or anyone who cares to know), faith tells us that Christ is ever-present (body, soul, and divinity) within the Consecrated Host in the Blessed Sacrament Tabernacle. During my adoration of the Blessed Sacrament, Jesus never fails to let me know He is there with me, through the peace and joy that I depart with no matter what heaviness I arrived with. I implore you, make an appointment with the Lord today: "Approach His throne of grace with confidence to receive grace and mercy to help you in your time of need" (Heb. 4:16). Go on; God's grace is sufficient for you (2 Cor. 12:9). Worship God like you never did before—that is the secret. Expect to weather any storm in His presence with His divine strength.

One day, I was listening to a Christian Television (TBN)[iv] program and a lady was giving testimony about how she lost her job and everything she had and became homeless. As she reached the end of her rope, she yearned for God and began to seek the face of God.

She asked God for a word on what to do next, and the Lord answered her prayer. From that point on, she said, she began to seek the Lord in all she did, and the Lord blessed her in more ways than she could imagine. The aftermath of her suffering and yielding to God's leading resulted in her becoming a multimillionaire eventually. The bottom line was that, had she not lost her job and gone through the humbling wilderness and purification experiences, she would not be a millionaire today.

God is ever with us and in control, but we must be still to know He is around, and trust Him to realize what He is doing. One fateful day before work as I have shared the story before, I went to the church for morning Mass and became emotionally engulfed in a feeling of victimization. I was angry, upset, and confused, but I drew strength from God's presence in the Tabernacle. As I prayed through tearful eyes, I longed for His comforting arm and wished He could speak to me. In the afternoon, I came back to the office and my voicemail message light was on. A friend of mine had left me this message: "Rejoice always, pray without ceasing, in all circumstances give thanks, for this is the will of God for you in Christ Jesus" (1 Thess. 5:16–18).

I cried even more, because I knew that I had just heard from God. He wanted me to cheer up and keep praying and trusting. I resumed my work feeling better and convinced that the Lord was still in control. But He was not yet done with me! That evening after I got home, God taught me another lesson in life and asked me to forgive all my adversaries and forget the old hurts. His message was very clear and direct. He told me not to depend on myself or on others anymore, but to look upon Him for all my needs. He wanted me to offer my trials and tribulations to Him for the forgiveness of sins while waiting patiently on His promises. This experience gave me new hope and a new understanding of the phrase "God is in control."

Don't think He has forgotten you. Ask Him; listen and wait for Him to speak; He will speak to you when you least expect it. He is aware of your every pain and wants to take it away, if only you can ask and allow Him to lead you. I can testify from my own journey that God provides for us physically, financially, and spiritually when we yield to His leading. I can tell you that there was a period when I did not know how the bills were paid. God provided for my basic needs and fed me like a raven. That is God for you.

My openness to trust in the Lord after that day opened up new possibilities for what God wanted from me. That same evening, I was filled with the uncontrollable urge to write down my thoughts as the Spirit ministered to me. I stopped feeling helpless; I felt overjoyed at His reassurance of the rewards for my obedience. I felt humbled by the opportunity to hear Him and minister to others using what He taught me. I learned that I didn't have to worry or be anxious about anything; I only needed to open my heart and allow the Holy Spirit to direct me to God through prayer, the Sacraments of the church for grace, and the Word of God for instructions.

So, if you're still wondering whether God can really turn things around for you as He did for me, relax; He has always been and will continue to be in control of your issues, no matter how big or small, if you let Him. It is never too late to have the kind of life you wish for, the marriage you've always dreamed about, children that you would be proud of, and the spiritual height you desire. You just have to surrender to Him with much love and trust through obedience while He works for you. God the "I AM" wants you to know that He loves you and that *love* is the pathway to Him.

Despair, or undermining God's unconditional love, is the

devil's advocate and desire. The devil exploits our vulnerability when we let down our guards. That is when we stop praying, become distracted from studying the Bible, lose faith or trust in God, and begin to operate in the flesh. By relying on the knowledge that He loves us, even with our imperfections, we thwart the enemy's plans to make us feel worthless, victimized, condemned, and discouraged. Our call is to be sincere in our resolve to love, serve, and trust God, and He will help us to overcome weakness and anguish when we stay close to Him. I understood that I don't have to carry the weight of my problems on my shoulder; I have an advocate and a helper who is eager to take it over.

In the message of February 5, 2011, given to Maria Divine Mercy (MDM) and titled "Love Is the Way to Salvation," Jesus invited us to surrender and hand over our worries to Him saying:

> "It is only through prayer and by handing Me over your troubles that you will become in union with Me. When you surrender My daughter, and trust in Me then you will understand the love I hold for you in My heart. And when you do, your love for Me will grow stronger. It is only when you offer up all your concerns and place them in My hands that they will be taken care of."[v]

As I continued to write, my spirit was lifted to praise the Lord. I found myself reading through the "love letter" I wrote to God in 2006, which is republished in this book to glorify God again, and again.

ALLOW ME TO TAKE OVER

He gives strength to the weary and increases the power of the weak...
Those who hope in the LORD will renew their strength. They will
soar on wings like eagles; they will run and not grow weary,
they will walk and not be faint.

(Isa. 40:29, 31)

Have you been praying for healing or a financial breakthrough? Have you lamented and prayed to God for a change of heart and attitude for you or a spouse, a child, relative, friend or even your boss? Do you keep giving and wondering when it will be your turn to be blessed? When you picked up this book, the title probably jumped right out at you because you can relate to it in one way or another, right? If so, are you getting, weary or discouraged and want God to take over because you are getting tired?

I know that God does not lie. Scripture tells us that the Lord will heal our broken hearts and bind up our wounds (Psa. 147:3). However, we get confused, dismayed, and despondent when bad things contrary to His promises happen to us. In the first place, God is infallible, and neither changes nor fails. And He would not start to change now because of you and me. In my case, I realized that God never deserted me, even though it seemed like it. Rather, the Lord delivered my soul from death, my eyes from tears, and my feet from stumbling when I submitted to Him. Ironically, our refusal to release total control to God despite handing the issues over to him in prayer renders Him powerless to take over.

Let me ask you: how would you feel if someone handed something to you but kept holding onto it, refusing to let go completely? Wouldn't you say to the person, "You're not serious, call me when you're ready for me to have it, or keep it until you're ready to let go"? Think about how God feels all the time when His children refuse to let go of the concerns and battles they hand over to Him. Until we come to the Father with confidence and love, like a child, and say to Him, "Daddy, I need this; Daddy, this person upsets me today; oh, Daddy, can you please show me how to do this?" and walk away carefree knowing that Daddy will get to it, we deny and disrespect the Father. He may not do it immediately, but because a child knows that Daddy or Mommy is the only provider and protector, the child is confident that everything will be okay.

That is why anyone who comes to God must be like a child before Him. What the Father wants from us is not as hard as it seems. Because all good virtues and righteousness (right living) come by grace through Christ Jesus, and so all we need to do is open our hearts to Him, and approach Him with the humility and confidence of a child. It is never by power! The Lord, according to 2 Chron. 16:9, is looking around throughout the earth for receivers who are disposed to receive. Those who love God receive by faith, humility, and obedience, and find solutions to their needs. Unfortunately, many people do not know they are the obstacles to their own solutions and breakthroughs.

In one of the messages to MDM, given on August 17, 2011, titled "How to Ask Me to Help You Resolve Your Worries", Jesus drove home my point when He said:

"Confidence in Me children is very important. Yes it brings

much joy to My sacred heart when I feel your love for me. However it is only when you truly confide in Me and let go of all your worries by passing them over to me, so I can take care of them, that you can only feel a sense of true peace. So many of My children pray for special intentions. I listen to every single one. But you must, when praying to Me for something very important to you, let go of your fears. Fear is not from Me. It is given to you by Satan as a means to torment you. Don't you understand this? When you fear something which you feel has a grip over your life, the more you fear, the more the problem festers."[vi]

The Lord emphasizes the need for us to let go for His will to be done. Continuing the words of the message, He said:

"It is only when you stop and say to Me Jesus, I hand you over all my concerns in this matter in confidence so that the problem is now yours to resolve according to your most Holy Will" that your mind can be at peace. This is what I mean by confidence children. Confidence in Me means that you display a great trust. Trust in Me. I died for your sins—every single one of you alive today even in this age. Why would you not trust in Me? I love you like no other creature on this earth. No one will or can love you like I do."

Often in moments of crisis and helplessness, human beings run to God to offload. But after everything goes back to normal, self-will kicks in to take back control, and we take God off our priority list again as He, God, sits and watches from the outside to allow us exercise our free will. We go back to living like "nothing mega," no shaking! At other times, we want God to take over, but we're not sure if He can handle it as quickly as we expect or want it. The worst are people who want God to take control, but shut Him out by refusing to give Him attention. I wonder how many of us can handle that?

We shut God out and make him unable to take control in the following situations: (1) when we become overly distracted by the quest for material things and take our eyes off Jesus; (2) when we worry, fear, doubt, or murmur in our hearts against God, which translates to lack of faith and a vote of no confidence in Him; (3) when our minds and hearts are heavily clouded by jealousy, envy, bitterness, anger, resentment, etc.; (4) whenever we look to other human beings, ourselves, or other sources for solutions rather than to God the Creator; and (5) when we idolize created things instead of the Creator and fail to acknowledge Him in all we do and for all He has done.

Those who know the God they serve have come to understand that the secret to having peace and freedom is taking the Father's hand while walking one step at a time in His footsteps. And the secret to pleasing Him is praising your way out of any situation while giving thanks in all circumstances. In so doing, you are not only bonding with your heavenly Father, you are also letting Him know you care; and, at the same time, disposing yourself to receive from Him. For he says: "And I, when I am lifted up from the earth, will draw all people to myself."(Jn. 12:32)

Those who know how to enter His court through praise and worship and know how to open their mouths to declare the Word of God will have no need to fear. They, according to Philippians 4:6 will not fret or have anxiety about anything, but in every circumstance and in everything, by prayer and petition, with thanksgiving; will make known their requests to God. And the Lord's peace that transcends all understanding shall guard their hearts and minds, and they will have no room to dwell in doubt or worry. (Phil. 4:7)

When you find time for the Lord and engage Him in praise and worship, you are showing Him reverent love and devotion; therefore, ushering in His glory, mercy, favors, and graces. His Word says, "If I were hungry I would not tell you, for the world is mine and all it contains… He who offers a sacrifice of thanksgiving honors Me; and to him who orders his way aright I shall show the salvation of God" (Psa. 50:12, 23). I will talk about this kind of worship in more detail, but first understand that you can only be a true worshiper if you love God; otherwise, it would be a struggle for you. You can only give what you have. If you don't love the Lord in truth, you can't offer Him acceptable worship.

I would like to shed more light on my worship experience for those that are new to it. Worshiping God in truth and in spirit reveals His presence whenever you are in doubt. It is a personal, one-on-one experience when you come into the glorious presence of God with praises and thanksgiving, in adoring and esteem devotion that show honor and love for God. It is not the usual church Sunday worship that I am referring to now, though it could happen in the church or group worship if you are keyed in the spirit. You begin by inviting the Holy Spirit to come into your heart and take over. In His presence, recognize that you are a sinner and confess your sins of omission and commission asking God for forgiveness and mercy. He says: "If we confess our sins, He is faithful and righteous to forgive us our sins and to cleanse us from all." (1 Jn. 1:9)

You worship and praise God with songs and words of exaltation, glorifying Him for who He is and all He has done. As you worship, you can address Him by His holy names referenced in Scripture (Omnipotent, Omnipresent, Alpha & Omega, Jehovah Jireh, Adonai, Jehovah Rapha, El-Shaddai, Elohim, etc.) and as you wish. I like to call him the "Wind" beneath my wings. Without fear, open up yourself completely and speak to Him as a child about everything—your fears, worries, pains, concerns, struggles, needs, fantasies, desires, dreams and plans, etc. In adoration worship, miracles of the heart happen; the Holy Spirit begins to break cold, bitter, and hardened hearts, filling them with His Spirit of forgiveness, love, peace, joy, humility, etc. In praise and worship, heaven opens and the glory of God comes down with grace to strengthen you.

Make this time with God special; pay Him homage in humility and docility and cry out to Him as your Helper, and the Lover of your soul. For where the Spirit of God is-- in His presence, there is liberty (2 Cori. 3:17) and anointing that destroys yokes (Isa. 10:27). If you are led to enter into prophetic singing (which is singing your prayers as an act of adoration and appreciation to God), don't hold back! And if you are led to pray in the Spirit or a strange language (tongue), open your mouth and speak; don't be embarrassed! The key is to allow the disposition of your mind and spirit to connect and yield to the Holy Spirit.

In praise and worship devotion; during the adoration of God in the Blessed Sacrament and, every time you come into His glorious presence in prayers, you are saying to God "take over." You are acknowledging your dependency on Him and your inability to do more for yourself. You are taking His hands and learning how to walk beside Him and not before Him. After all, Scripture says in Jeremiah 29:11 that His plan for you is better than what you have in mind; plans to prosper you and not to harm you, plans to give you hope and a future.

Finally, once you invite God into your heart and into your situations, allow Him to take full control by the show of faith and, believe without fear or doubt that He is able to do above and beyond all that you ask or think through His mighty power at work within you

(Eph. 3:20), according to His will. I can guarantee from experience, God will rise to the occasion if you allow Him.

ALLOW ME TO LEAD YOU

I will instruct you and teach you in the way you should go;
I will counsel you and watch over you. Do not be like the horse
or the mule, which have no understanding but must be
controlled by bit and bridle...

(Ps. 32:8-9)

Do you ever think that the Holy Spirit doesn't speak to you, or want to speak to you? If so, why won't He? Why wouldn't He want to speak to us if He expects us to be led by Him? God does speak to His children, but you have to be still to hear His quiet voice speak to your heart. He gives us directions and speaks to us in different ways (dreams, visions, the Bible and spiritual books, intuition, events around us, and more), but we often miss it when we are not united with Him in spirit.

Even though God is with us, He appears far from us when we don't seek Him. By the same token, God appears silent when we are not tuned in. For instance, when you are very busy with everything else and unable to pray, read the Bible, or spend quality time with God, it becomes harder to hear His still voice. We can also shut out the still voice of warning when we come to Him expecting to hear only what we want to hear. Jesus desires to lead us, but we have to be sensitive to know when He speaks, and be still to hear His voice.

I perceive the Holy Spirit ministering to my spirit as I write: My children, allow Me to lead you to My heart where you will find rest. Let Me guide and direct you on this journey as you struggle daily to please Me. I, your Jesus, would like to lead you, protect you, teach you, and show you the way—the right way, the truth, and the life. For long have I waited for your love, to hold you and put my arms around you as My little children, dry up your tears, and take away your fears. Do you not know that I hurt when you hurt; I flinch and reach out my hands when you fall. I carry you when it becomes too difficult for you alone to walk. I am your loving Savior, and as the Father has loved Me, so have I loved you. Now remain in My love (John 15:9).

Putting these words on the paper made my eyes teary. All that afternoon I perceived the Holy Spirit pouring into my spirit even as I go about my daily activities. He desires to make a personal appeal to every heart who will hear. God loves you and wants something better for you than you are currently experiencing, because His plans for you are good. It is only a good father who corrects his children and will not spare the rod lest the child become rotten or useless to him. As I see it, God allowed me to go through purification and crisis to prepare me and equip me for His greater calling and purpose.

If life were all hunky-dory-donkey and everything were perfect, most people would have forgotten about God by now, because there would be no need for Him. Think about it. Yet God wants so much to have a personal relationship with us based on mutual love. When you submit to His leading, the LORD will guide you always; he will satisfy your needs in a sun-scorched land and will strengthen your frame. You will be like a well-watered garden, like a spring whose waters never fail" (Isaiah 58:11). Why not submit to His leading?

In my life, I have come to appreciate the leading of the Holy Spirit, maybe because I've experienced the consequences of going off on my own. One of my prayer partners always tells me that before she does anything, she asks the Holy Spirit to show her what to do and how to do it. She said she depends so much on the Holy Spirit (our teacher) that even when she needs a good spot in a crowded parking lot, she asks the Holy Spirit and He has never failed. One day I decided to try asking the Holy Spirit to hold my appointment slot at my doctor's office, because once you are five minutes late with this office, you'd better reschedule. I was shocked to be ushered into the doctor's room 30 minutes late that day, just because I asked the Holy Spirit to keep my appointment. You may think this is nothing, but it was much to me. To God, the small and the big stuff are the same anyhow.

"Here I am," says the Lord, "I stand at the door [of your heart] and knock; if anyone hears My voice and opens, I will come in and eat with him" (Rev. 2:20). To answer is to humble yourself before God, and be willing even if you fall flat on your face trying. God is not expecting a perfect or sinless soul, but the desire of a simple and willing heart. It is His Spirit that enables us not to give up or be discouraged by our failures and weaknesses. Therefore, for God to lead us, we must trust in His mercy and allow His joy to be our strength, for it is through intimacy with Christ that we are able to live right.

To be led by the Holy Spirit, you will have to invite Him daily to come in and literally be part of all you do. You allow Him to drive while you are in the passenger's seat listening and trusting. Once the Holy Spirit is in you, He breaks down walls of resistance and supplies the grace for holiness and for breakthroughs. So, do not let your heart be troubled, but trust in God to lead you to places you would never be able to reach on your own; He knows the way and will never mislead you. Intoxication with the Holy Spirit leads one's spirit to a continuous subconscious worship of God even while sleeping or driving.

The Lord offers us a life devoid of pain and lack if we agree to be led by Him. If we accept His offer, then we have freedom, joy, and happiness; if we reject His Spirit in us, then we struggle and suffer. As you begin to open your heart to Him, He shows you the way and guides you on the path to follow. But you can't ask God to lead and refuse to follow, or claim to know the way and expect to be led—God hates a prideful soul! You have to be teachable, humble, and open to be led by the Holy Spirit. In summary, to be led by God is to submit to His will in all areas of your life with unwavering faith.

To end this chapter, let me share with you a message of encouragement given to MDM on January 8, 2012 in which Jesus reveals to us what pleases Him in simple language[vii]:

My dearest beloved daughter, I call out today to all children over the age of seven and to every single child of mine in the world. You, my little children, are like jewels in My Eyes. You bring Me such tender love and I delight in your company. Know that I love you very much. Some of you know Me already and that is good. I invite you to chat with me more in your own words as a friend. Never feel you must learn or recite prayers, which you may find difficult. Instead come to Me and share all of your thoughts, fears, news or problems. I am always at your side even when you ignore Me. I am always hopeful.

To those poor young people whose lives are filled with falsities or who are involved with drink or drugs you must know this. Although you may feel emptiness inside, you must give Me your hand and I will grasp it. I will save you from drowning in a sea of confusion. Many of you feel worthless and of no significance. You are so overwhelmed by those you idolize in the world of music and celebrity that you feel completely inadequate. Never feel like this my little children because, in My Eyes, you are very special. Each of you holds a unique place in My Heart. Allow Me to take you on a journey to a wonderful new future. I will, shortly, introduce a new wonderful Era of Peace and Glory on earth. You must keep strong. Never give up when you feel down.

Never despair when you feel worthless. You, remember, were born for a reason. No matter what your circumstances are, the reason for your birth is this. You were born to join with Me as part of My New Glorious Kingdom. I know it is hard for you to hear My Voice as there are so many false gods trying to get your attention. My promise to you is this. Live your life in hope and love for me, your Jesus, and I will give you the gift of Paradise. This Paradise is what is waiting for you if you would only ask Me to help you on your journey towards Me.

I am the love that is missing from your life.

I am the peace you look for.

I am the help you need to feel love in your heart again.

I am Love. I am the Light. Without Me you will remain in darkness.

I love you no matter how you may hurt Me or offend Me.

Rejoice, My children, because I now speak to your heart from the Heavens.

I am real. I exist.

I love you and I will never give up my fight to save you so that I can take you, your family and friends to the New Paradise on Earth.

This Paradise was created for Adam and Eve and will now return to earth. I want you to be part of this new Glorious life, which is beyond your dreams. I bless you now.

Your beloved friend, Jesus

Now say this little prayer and I will come running to you immediately:

Jesus, if you can hear me
Then listen to my call for help
Please help me deal with those who cause me pain
Help me to stop envy taking over my life and
To stop me wishing for things I cannot have
Instead open my heart to you, dear Jesus
Help me to feel real love—Your love
And to feel true peace in my heart. Amen.

ALLOW ME TO HEAL YOU

For I will restore you to health And I will heal you of your wounds,"
declares the LORD, "Because they have called you an outcast,
saying: 'It is Zion; no one cares for her.

(Jer. 30:17)

The Bible's promises of health and healing are many, and we stand by it in authority to assert and claim our healing. When Christ went to the cross 2,000 years ago, "He took our illnesses and bore our diseases" (Matt. 8:14-17), He was wounded for our transgressions, He was bruised for our iniquities; the chastisement for our peace was upon Him, and by His stripes we are healed (Isa. 53:5). Since the Word of God has assured us that healing is our portion, the question is: why are we not in good health? Why are we, the redeemed and healed of the Lord, still not healed from physical and mental infirmities?

As I understood it, even though healing has been accomplished by Christ for us, you still have to believe and receive it with faith. To believe, you have to constantly hear and apply the healing words (Scriptures) by faith as your authority to be healed. Consequently, faith comes from hearing the message--through the word of God (Rom. 10:17). The word of God is medicinal and gives healing to the body and soul. The Lord says: "My son, pay attention to what I say; listen closely to My Words. Do not let them out of your sight, keep them within your heart; for they are life to those who find them and health to a man's whole body." (Prov. 4: 20-22). The Word of God confessed and declared with authority and faith brings healing.

"But I have done all that before, Cathy, and still not healed." Don't worry! Apart from the instantaneous miraculous healing that can happen anytime by the exhibition of a strong faith, please understand that healing is a gradual process that occurs as long as you keep believing and applying the principles of positive confession of the healing Words of God over and over, irrespective of what your body feels, while still taking good care of your body and soul.

Secondly, healing is as much a spiritual thing as it is a physical thing. Every infirmity that manifests itself as sickness in one's life has a spirit behind it which comes with hindrances and baggage that block healing from manifestation. So until those blocking elements are done away with (spiritual healing), the physical manifestation is delayed. Lastly, praying the will of God in every situation pulls you through the difficult time of suffering; especially, when you have done all you are supposed to do spiritually and medically. While still believing God on His promises for your healing, offer God your pains and sufferings; and that way, your suffering will not be in vain.

I can imagine Jesus saying: "I wish above all things that you prosper and be in health, even as your soul prospered" (3 John 2). "I am the Lord who heals you" (Ex. 15:26). Allow Me to heal your physical sufferings, but above all, allow Me to heal not only your body but your mind and soul as well. Know that the healing, which was completed for you on Calvary, will manifest in the body only when the spiritual is healed and healthy, and you believe that it is done. Come to Me with your prayer of faith, for the prayer offered in faith will make the sick person well; and I the Lord will raise them up. If they have sinned, they will be forgiven (James 5:15).

It is important to bear in mind that God's promises of healing for you also apply to anyone you pray for with faith. He commissioned us with healing authority, according to James 5: "Is any one of you sick? He should call the elders of the church to pray over him and anoint him with oil in the name of the Lord. Therefore confess your sins to each other and pray for each other so that you may be healed. The prayer of a righteous man is powerful and effective" (James 5:14, 16). The elders could be any believer(s) with faith, for "truly if two of you agree here on earth concerning anything you ask, my Father in heaven will do it for you" (Matt. 18:19).

When you pray for healing, always confess your sins to God and ask for forgiveness. Reason with the Lord for "Though your sins are like scarlet, they shall be as white as snow" says the Lord (Isa. 1:18)." With your mouth, according to what I learnt in a healing service retreat, renounce every spirit associated with your sickness. For example, you can say, "I renounce you, evil spirit of diabetes, eating disorders, and bulimia. I reject and renounce you, spirit of cancer, un-forgiveness, bitterness, etc." Next, command the infirmity to leave your body, casting it out in the name of Jesus. Say, "I command you, spirit of ___, to leave my body now in the name of Jesus." Then break the powers of all the spirits you renounced and cast out: "I break your powers over my life, you evil spirit of ____, in the name of Jesus." Pray with faith and believe with conviction over and over that you are healed.

The biggest obstacle to healing is a refusal to forgive. If you don't know by now, know it now! Yes, Jesus asked us to forgive everyone (not forgive and hang on to it). And I believe that He was very clear when he said in Luke 6:37, "Do not judge and you will not be judged. Do not condemn, and you will not be condemned. Forgive, and you will be forgiven." Think about the Lord's Prayer: what you are saying to God is "Lord, forgive me my sins against you, and I promise to forgive those that sinned against me, okay?" If God took you up on your promise and forgave you as many times as you asked, and you didn't keep your own end of the agreement, you lied!

The way I understood it now, forgiveness is not about the person that offended you, but about your obedience. You shortchange yourself when you don't forgive, because the devil will always use your lack of forgiveness against you before God when you pray, and God can't go against His Word; too bad for the one who cannot let it go. To put it mildly, you risk not being healed or not receiving an answer to your prayers until you can release that person or persons through forgiveness. The day I made up my mind that no one was worth blocking my blessings was the day I won the victory.

Funny, I remember somebody mocking me because I extended a greeting to my ex-husband at a party not long after he lied about me for his selfish gain. Yes, I was able to forgive him that fast, because I did it not for him, but for me. God said, "If you love Me, you will obey Me" (John 14:23). I would rather be seen as stupid or weak than disobey God and lose my blessings. Bitterness, anger, jealousy, and envy are all obstacles to healing. To be healed means to be set free from physical, mental, emotional, and spiritual infirmities. You have to get rid of extra baggage to be free.

A Catholic healing priest shared a testimony about a religious woman who had devoted her life to the service of God, but suffered from a spinal cord injury that had defied prayer to the point that she became bedridden. According to the priest who prayed for her healing and gave the testimony, it was a case of healing blocked by a lack of forgiveness for years. When the priest was invited to pray for her, the Lord led him to ask her if there was anyone she needed to forgive. She said yes and burst into tears. The priest then led her through forgiveness and renouncing prayers as she went down memory lane, openly forgiving each person by name.

Two days after the prayers, the priest received a call to come back to the bed of the woman, and guess who jumped out of bed completely and totally healed? Praise God! It turned out that she had held a grudge against her father for many years due to some kind of abuse, and that kept her crippled physically as well as spiritually for a long time and denied this servant of God her healing.

At the retreat given by this same priest[viii], I picked up three principles of prayer power that can be used especially when praying for healing:

1. **Power of Agreement Prayer:** "Again, truly I tell you that if two of you on earth agree about anything they ask for, it will be done for them by my Father in heaven. And where two or three gather in my name, there I am with them" (Matt. 18:19-20). There is power in agreement prayer, especially when you lay hands on a sick person as a group of family members, church, or prayer partners and agree by faith that the person is healed.

2. **Power of a True Worshiper--One Who Worships God in spirit with Songs of Praise and Thanksgiving:** "But an hour is coming, and now is, when the true worshipers will worship the Father in spirit and truth; for such people the Father seeks to be His worshipers" (John 4:23). I have heard countless numbers of testimonies about healing received as a result of praising God in the midst of bad situations, and the power of praise and worship to make the impossible possible.

3. **Power of Praying in Jesus' Name**: "And these signs will

accompany those who believe: In my name, they will drive out demons; they will speak in new tongues" (Mark 16:17). "At the name of Jesus, every knee shall bow, in heaven and on earth and under the earth" (Phil. 2:10). We pray in the name of Jesus to assert our authority in Christ. And Jesus himself asked us to pray in His name: "And I will do whatever you ask in my name, so that the Father may be glorified in the Son" (John 14:13).

Prayer for healing has been scientifically proven to work. I read recently about a scientific study where a team of researchers went out to the scientific and medical community to learn the potential benefits of prayer.[ix] Per the report, what they found out both surprised and excited all of them. Their findings, as reported by Newsmax, revealed the following:

- How a specific amount of "prayer time" per day can help prevent memory loss, mental decline, and even dementia or Alzheimer's.

- 47 scientifically proven benefits of prayer, including pain relief, reduced risk of death from heart attack or stroke, lessened anxiety or depression, and more . . .

In addition to the power of prayers, think about the power of fasting, almsgiving and obedience when you are praying and believing for healing. While fasting by abstinence is powerful when your health allows it, Isaiah 58 summoned up the kind of fasting we should be mindful:

"Is not this the kind of fasting I have chosen: to loose the chains of injustice and untie the cords of the yoke, to set the oppressed free and break every yoke? Is it not to share your food with the hungry and to provide the poor wanderer with shelter—when you see the naked, to clothe them, and not to turn away from your own flesh and blood? Then your light will break forth like the dawn and your healing will quickly appear; then your righteousness[a] will go before you, and the glory of the Lord will be your rear guard. Then you will call, and the Lord will answer; you will cry for help, and he will say: Here am I" (Isa. 58:6-9).

Above all, it is essential to do all within your power to live at peace with others. In conclusion, please receive this gift of healing message and prayer from Jesus with an open mind; given to MDM on January 15, 2013:

My dearly beloved daughter, as this Mission continues to grow and expand around the world, it will come with new miracles, which, in My compassion, will be given to those who suffer terribly. When I came the first time, My Mercy was extended to those souls who needed My Help. There will be those who will be infiltrated by a lack of faith and who will be afflicted by terrible physical suffering. Those who come to Me, I will ease their suffering. I will do this to ignite the faith of their souls, but it will be by the Power of the Holy Spirit, by which they can only be healed. Bring Me your sufferings. Bring Me your worries. Bring Me your pain. Come to Me, through your prayers, and I will listen. I wish to take you all in My Sacred Arms and protect you.

Please take this new Gift of Healing I present to you now. It is in the form of a Crusade Prayer and will cure you in mind, body and soul. By this prayer, I bequeath the precious Gift of Healing. By reciting it you will know that this request for help will bring down upon you, and those you include in this prayer, great gifts from Heaven. As such, it comes with a special protection for the renewal of those lost, who are unsure of their faith, and who feel a sense of weariness. They may be suffering from doubts. They may be suffering with physical diseases, which are destroying their ability to allow Me to bring them peace, love and comfort.

To receive this blessing for healing please recite this Crusade Prayer to cure the mind, body and soul:

O dear Jesus, I lay myself before You, weary, sick, in pain and with a longing to hear Your Voice. Let me be touched by Your Divine Presence, so that I will be flooded by Your Divine Light through my mind, body and soul.

I trust in Your Mercy.

I surrender my pain and suffering completely before You and I ask that You give me the grace to trust in You, so that You can cure me of this pain and darkness, so that I can become whole again and, so that I can follow the Path of Truth and allow You to lead me to life in the New Paradise. Amen

It is your faith that must concern you, first. Then, by the grace of My Mercy, will I respond to your request for healing, according to My Holy Will.

Your beloved Jesus.[x]

ALLOW ME TO CHANGE YOU AND CHANGE HIM/HER FOR YOU

Trust in the LORD with all your heart. Never rely
On what you think you know. Remember the LORD in
everything you do and He will show you the right way

(Prov. 3:5–6)

Sometimes it takes a painful experience to make us change our ways, but it doesn't have to. It's God's wish that we draw near to Him by the desires of our own hearts, so that it is not only trials, hardships, and crises that force us to turn to Him. As I have previously said, God allows us to go through purification by suffering and crisis so we can be rewired (change of heart, attitude, and thought process) and renewed by the experiences, to His glory and for our benefit. Because I lived through it, I can stand to testify to it.

God knows that as long as we are in the flesh, we are susceptible and prone to sin. Even the most pious believers and shepherds of God's flock struggle with sin and weakness. St. Paul in Romans 7:15 said, "I do not understand what I do. For what I want to do I do not do, but what I hate I do." When we walk in the flesh (worldly or carnal-minded) by following the desires of our own hearts and ways, we wander out of His presence and grace, and manifest jealousy, strife, envy, and bitterness as the fruits of carnal-mindedness. Yet our Lord's patience is unprecedented and His love inexhaustible.

While we may love God too and want to please Him, unfortunately, it is the forces behind the spirit of the flesh that antagonize God and influence all negative actions in us. For the Scriptures say, "Those who are in the flesh cannot please God" (Rom. 8:8). The flesh fights us ruthlessly through distractions to deny us the presence of God and prevent us from loving Him as we were created to. Only in Christ Jesus can we walk in uprightness and love unconditionally. Jesus said, "I am the vine, you are the branches: he, who is in me at all times as I am in him, bears much fruit, because without me you are able to do nothing. If you are in me and my words are in you, then anything for which you make a request will be done for you" (John 15:5, 7).

Draw near to God and He will draw near to you (James 4:8). As you do, His Spirit active in you will gradually break the walls of resistance, melt away every pain, and loose the hardened heart, while supplying a fresh aroma of grace into you to live and love as He intended for you. Only then does change become easy, as you begin to notice that you are no longer getting upset over little stuff like you used to. Your patience and tolerance levels begin to increase as grace multiplies. It is a good feeling knowing that you are no longer controlled by the flesh and your ability to say no to "evil" and yes to "good" also increases. That is when you know that it is God making the changes in you.

Our Lord Jesus in a message to MDM on June 21, 2012, entitled Come to Me All of You Who Feel Unworthy have this to say:

While I will chastise you for any wrongdoing, and become angry when you do evil onto others; while I will never let you wander off the path of Truth without coaxing you back to Me; and, while I will never give you everything you ask for unless it is according to My

Most Holy Will; yet: I am patient. I am not easily shocked and never, nor could I, hold a grudge. I am waiting for you. Our Lord continued in His appeal to us:

So many people are lost and have forgotten Me. Many, because of the sinful lives they have led, are reluctant to turn to Me. They feel awkward, don't know how to pray and believe, wrongly, that it is too late for them. How wrong they are. They must never forget that I offered up My life on earth for each one of you. I don't give up on souls that easily. I love all those who, through their actions, deeds and thoughts, break My Father's Laws. You are precious to Me. I love you just as I love all of God's children. Never believe you are loved less because you sin. Sin, while abhorrent to Me, is the stain with which you were born. It is almost impossible for any soul on earth not to sin. Never feel I could never help you or welcome you into My Arms.[xi]

Yes, God supplies the grace to walk in love and live by the fruits of the Spirit. "The fruit of the Spirit is love, joy, peace, forbearance, kindness, goodness, gentleness, faithfulness, patience, and self-control, against such things there is no law" (Gal. 5:22-23). "Not by might, but by my Spirit" (Zech. 4:6), says the Lord; therefore, only the Holy Spirit reforms, transforms, renews, and purifies both you and others whom you wish to change to walk in victory. Intimacy with God through frequenting the Sacraments; especially, Holy Eucharist and reconciliation, praying and meditating on the Scripture daily reproduces more graces.

Willingness to change is a self-decision while ability to change comes by grace. When you are not willing to admit that you have an issue, change eludes you. When in doubt, seek His wisdom in prayer and you can never go wrong. Fear the Lord and consider Him first before you act and in all you do. Say to yourself especially when tempted, "If not for God, I would have or wouldn't have…" The reward is with the Father! When it comes to decision time, ask the Lord what He will have you do. Catholics invoke our Blessed Mother's intercession and help through the Rosary and Divine Mercy prayers; her maternal instinct will draw you closer to her Son.

Some people who struggle with addiction and vice actually believe they have been overpowered and will never be able to overcome the addiction. That is true only if you believe it. What you believe and confess is what you will get. For instance, I have tried overcoming the weakness of being late to church but failed, because I kept confessing that I was never able to get there on time, so the devil capitalized on my confession and held me hostage to being late. One morning, my Spirit told me that I could reject that lie and confess instead that I could be early, because Philippians 4:13 says that I can do all this through Him who gives me strength.

To successfully change or expect change on someone else for that matter, be humble enough to recognize your own weaknesses and faults and want to do something about it. If you believe you don't have a fault and people close to you are saying otherwise; take it as a hint and go to God with what they are saying. Be open to what the Holy Spirit will reveal, and to the changes He desires, if they are right. For instance, many couples in marriage relationships feel that if only one spouse could change, everything would be okay. Really! But that is not how God sees it. It is difficult to change one self, but it is twice as difficult to change someone else. Trust me, I know—or go ask anyone in a difficult relationship.

The Bible says to remove the log from your eye before you remove the mote from your brother's eye (Matt. 7:5). I am not undermining anyone's anguish in a bad relationship because I have been there. I am just saying that the Lord will always wait on you to do the right thing yourself. I believe that after you show an honest desire and willingness for change to start with you, the Lord will perfect the changes in your spouse.

Let the changing of your spouse (or anyone you are presenting to the Lord to change) be not by words; rather, let it be in actions through the selfless show of unconditional love, achieved through prayers and constant forgiveness. When you complained bitterly to God concerning someone's attitude, stop and listened, the Holy Spirit might be saying; "Lay him/her at My altar (pray for them) and allow Me to change and save their soul in my own way and time." In the process of praying for change in someone else, invite and allow God to change or straighten you as well. The change may be for you to see and handle what you have to deal with differently.

The Lord wants us to allow Him to do the changing. His desires would be to change our approach and renew us to become the stronger person in the relationship, full of love, patience, compassion, and tolerance for the other person. The same can be true when you desire a change for your child, a relative, a friend, or anyone else. Your part is to pray for them and continue to be faithful in your own duties and responsibilities to them, with love, instead of returning fire for fire or evil for evil. Believe me, I know, it's not that easy. There will be times when you feel like giving up, especially when it seems like you are giving so much and getting nothing back, not even appreciation.

Don't worry, and don't give up. It is at such times that the devil tests your strength by manipulating that person to drive you even more nuts. Satan is on a mission to destroy families, to fight God's authority on Earth. Don't let him deprive you of your inheritance. If you open the door and window, Satan will come in and dine with your family. Remember Job in the Bible? God allowed him to be tested for His glory, and in the end, He blessed Job abundantly for keeping faith. I did not give up praying, but unfortunately, in my case, the devil got a better hold on my ex and denied him an undeserved gift from God.

Be patient with yourself and with others, especially those you want to change. Change requires time, patience, prayer commitment, and constant communication. Don't push too hard, or you will defeat the purpose you are trying to achieve. I still believe that a man or woman who understands the importance of running to God to seek guidance will be richly blessed with wisdom, knowledge, and understanding, and clothed with divine strength to achieve anything. Such a person can reduce big issues to little stuff, and demolish strongholds and obstacles with the power of prayer, love, and forgiveness.

Finally, here is a message from November 24, 2010, titled "Stairway to Spiritual Perfection." Meditate on it and be encouraged by it in your own spiritual struggles. The message said:

Write this My beloved daughter. Faith has a way of deserting My most devout followers when they least expect it. This is important as it tests their faith so that they will come back into My heart all the more strong for the experience. Fear not, this is a trial which I allow My children to endure so that they will become stronger. It is not easy to retain your faith in Me, My children, as there are so many obstacles which block your devotion. You will, from time to time, feel a complete emptiness in your soul. This can leave you in an agitated state because you feel alone without a crutch.

For My faithful followers you must understand this. I, despite the loneliness you may experience, am never far away. All of these episodes have one goal, to strengthen your faith in a way so as to ensure that you move a new step towards Me each time. This is what is called the stairway to spiritual perfection that is Heaven. It is a long stairway and can take a very long time to reach the upper steps. Each step can represent a new revelation into what lessons you must experience before you can attain the graces you need to elevate your souls to the spiritual perfection needed to enter My Father's Paradise.

As each step is mounted a new awareness of which I expect of you is realized. Hard at times. Unfair, it may seem, at other times. But for each step you climb the more astute you become in understanding the truth of My teachings. Some climb these steps quickly while others take their time. Some of My devout followers may lose courage and back one step, two steps or three at a time. This is natural. Others who move too quickly gain a confidence that convinces them they understand all spiritual matters. But this is the Deceiver's Way of making you believe and accept this false confidence.

All gifts bestowed on you can only come from Me. They are given to you, My faithful followers, out of My boundless love for you. You must never assume that because your faith is strong that this is all your doing. Yes, your faith may be strong because of your tenderness of heart. Yet this is also a gift from Me. You must, in order to reach the top step, be humble in your love for Me. Show virtue at all times.

Show confidence in your faith by all means as this is pleasing to Me. But never fall into the trap of believing you know the full mysteries of the Divine Realm. As humans born with original sin, only time will reveal these mysteries to you, My children. Strive always to accept everything even the trials I may send you, as a gift from Me. All my gifts are bestowed to make you strong in your love for Me. I am so very proud of all My children who believe in Me and show Me honor and respect. So that I can lift you up to the full glory of My Father's Paradise you need to aspire to the glory of perfect union in Me.

To do this, My children, takes a little time and requires patience before you yield to the total abandonment of your soul to Me. Once that happens you become part of My mystical body for eternity. Surrender, My children, to My absolute pure love and you will never have to look back or fear for you will be safe in My arms. Keep strong, My faithful children even in the face of obstacles for I will never desert My beloved, devoted followers. Ever!

Your Loving Savior, Jesus Christ[xii]

ALLOW ME TO FIGHT YOUR BATTLES

Son, if you are going to serve the Lord, be prepared for times
when you will be put to the test. Be sincere and determined.
Keep calm when trouble comes. Stay with the Lord, never abandon
him, and you will be prosperous at the end of your days.

(Sir. 2:1–3)

Whoever says that being a believer (Christian) is easy is not giving you
the complete picture. Living a true Christian life is by grace and can be
achieved only if you understand the simplicity of God's desires, and
not the complexity of the many interpretations required. The
expectations of God's commandments may be hard for us when we
live outside the Spirit of God; controlled by our worldly desires, self-
will, and power. But as we learn to rely on God and surrender to His
will, we grow closer to Him in relationship. It becomes easier as we no
longer live for ourselves, but for Christ.

Being a true follower of Christ comes with persecution and
trials, according to the Bible: "If the world hates you, keep in mind that
it hated me first" (John 15:18). For, though we live in the world, we do
not wage war as the world does (2 Cor. 10:3-5). "Our struggle is not
against flesh and blood, but against the rulers, against the powers,
against the world forces of this darkness, against the spiritual forces of
wickedness in the heavenly places." (Eph. 6: 12). The good news is that
Christ has also made a way of escape for us by giving us the weapons
to fight our battles. He guaranteed us victory through Him as declared

in Jeremiah 1:19: "They will fight against you but will not overcome you, for I am with you and will rescue you," says the Lord.

Imagine being provoked and knowing that you can fight back, but because you love God and operate in the Spirit, turn to the Lord for justice. Imagine how you would dismantle your opponent, who would probably be expecting a fight at that point, and succeed in disgracing the demon forces behind that spirit of anger and revenge. Basically, the Word of God enjoins us to pursue peace at all costs. Even when we are oppressed, provoked, enraged, or attacked beyond our normal strength, instead of following our natural instincts to fight back in the flesh, we should turn the other cheek and hand over the battle to God.

My child, as I imagined what the Lord was saying in my case: Allow Me to fight this battle, for I alone give victory and delivers (Prov. 21:31). Is it not written that the battle is of the Lord (1 Sam. 17:47)? If you hand [him] and your persecutors over to Me and do not take revenge on your own, I will vindicate you. I will not allow shame to come to you, for no one who hopes in Me will ever be put to shame, but shame will come on those who are treacherous without cause (Prov. 25:3). Trust in Me, and hand over your battles (spiritual and physical) for I alone direct the heart of a king like a stream (Prov. 21:1). Those that persecute you, I will persecute, if you remain faithful to Me. Hand over your battles in obedience and be still and know that I am your God (Psa. 46:10).

There are two types of battles that we fight in the world: physical and spiritual. Physical battles are against opponents that we see with our naked eye (in the flesh). Spiritual battles are against spiritual powers, dominion, and wickedness in the high places (not seen with the naked eyes). However, before any battle is fought in the physical, chances are it has already been fought or is ongoing in the spiritual realm. Another kind of spiritual battle waged against us is "the battle of the mind" waged between good and evil in the mind. The Bible calls these adversaries the strongholds that torment our minds. Demons that instigate and control quarrel, rage and anger, jealousy, injustice, wickedness, and other vices operate inside their victims (mind) and use them to inflict pain on others.

The strongholds are the pretentious thoughts, false reasoning, and logical arguments of the world that are clearly against the truth and knowledge of God's Words. Satan's main purpose for waging war in our minds is to brew quarrels and confusion through distortions of truth, lies, and manipulation of reasoning and the Word of God. This battle must be won because the mind is where relationships and miracles are destroyed. Once the evil spirit succeeds in planting the seeds of fear and doubt in your mind, you will begin to wobble in your faith, and as noted before no double-minded person will receive anything from God (James 1:8). And when the seeds of discord—hatred, envy, jealousy, pride, bitterness, etc., are sown in the heart, relationships get destroyed.

This battle is instigated in the spiritual by the wicked spirits, and manifested physically through people who hurt, accuse, attack, oppress, or insult others with no justification, or with flimsy excuses. But Ephesians 6 encourages us to be strong in the Lord and in the strength of His might for our battles; to fight prepared with the full armor of God so that we will be able to stand firm against the schemes of the devil, and having done everything, to stand firm with the truth girding our loins in righteousness for breastplate; to march on with the gospel of peace; and to use faith as the shield with which to extinguish the flaming arrows of the evil one, and the Word of God as the sword of the Spirit (Eph. 6: 10-11, 13, 15-17).

The bottom line is that not all battles require our physical intervention. Through prayer, we can handle all spiritual battles, no matter how it manifests its face (injustice, racism, prejudice, insult, or injury), and no matter where it is coming from. Whether you believe the source to be an enemy you know or not, or from household watches or occult powers, stay clothed with the armor of God to withstand all evil.

Some people worry that letting things go in the physical means losing the battle, and maybe seen as a weakling. On the contrary, you win when you offer it up and hand it over to the Lord, who gives justice to the oppressed. He said: "Do not fear, for you will not be ashamed; do not be discouraged, for you will not suffer disgrace; for you will forget the shame of your youth, and the disgrace of your widowhood you will remember no more" (Isa. 54:4). One day, that person will look at you and wish he had the peace you have.

The first part of being able to not fight the physical battles is dealing with the spirit of pride and anger. The spirit behind "Do you know who I am?" or "I will deal with you." Yes, you may have the power to deal with the person, but do you have to? Not if you are to walk and win in Christ. Remember, it is not the one who started the fight that wins.

Important for spiritual warfare battle is praying on the Word of God, and standing in the righteousness of God in Christ Jesus to defend yourself and fire-back, otherwise your Holy Ghost fire will not burn anyone! For instance, if you struggle with the addictive sin of lust—lust of the flesh and lust of the eye (controlled by the demon forces and spirit against our homes and peace), your authority to bind and cast out an intruder from your life would be more effective after repentance, and with your resolve (by the help of God though prayers) to fight that evil spirit of lust holding you hostage. This should be your first warfare priority in order not to give the devil room to laugh at your prayers and throw it back at your face. "For everything in the world--the lust of the flesh, the lust of the eyes (greed), and the pride of life--comes not from the Father but from the world" (1 Jn. 2:16).

Before going into spiritual warfare prayer, always ask God for forgiveness, and declare the power of Romans 8:1-2: "For there is now no condemnation for those [me] who are in Christ Jesus, because through Christ the law of the Spirit who gives life has set me free from the law of sin and death." During spiritual warfare, stand on God's Words to reject evil programming and obstructions to your success, returning every arrow of affliction back to the sender. Cancel every bad dream and negative pronouncement against you with the Word of God; breaking its power in the name of Jesus. For instance, if you had an evil dream about death, you should stand on Psalm 118:17: "I will not die but live to testify to the goodness of the Lord" to cancel it.

Speak positive words about you, your children and your spouse because the power of life and death is in the tongue (Prov. 18:21). You also need faith to decree and declare a thing and believe your declaration will come to pass. So when you declare that no weapon formed against you shall prosper, you can live your life without fear, knowing that you are protected (Isa. 54:17).

Jesus wants us to start fighting a different kind of battle, with a different kind of weapon. The battle He wants us to engage now is the battle for souls. The battle for souls will be won through love, compassion, and prayers, even for enemies and unbelievers. The weapons are love, kindness, evangelism, and praying for souls. Seek to be empowered through wisdom and to demolish hatred, evil, and strongholds around you. Being nice to your adversary and responding with love when retaliation is expected can disarm your opponent and even make the person a believer by your actions, while you come up on top.

Finally, Jesus anguishes over how we treat each other. In a message given on November 25, 2010; entitled "Call on Believers to Convert Souls", He appealed to all of us:

My beloved loyal and devout followers are now, at this time, uniting around the world through the bond of powerful divine love to fight to save souls from damnation. These, My children of the light, come from all nations. They will recognize each other instantly irrespective of their race, color or creed. I am guiding them so that this army of love will help strengthen the faith of mankind at this point in history.

Never before have I made My presence so evident within the hearts of believers. They feel the suffering I endure as I witness the heart wrenching badness that emits from man even among those who you would deem to be kind and thoughtful. Love of self is destroying my children.

Selfishness and lack of consideration for those around you and for the vulnerable leaves a stain of shame that is hard to erase. The cruelty that man shows to his neighbor, all with one motive in mind—self-satisfaction, has reached an all-time high. The obsession with their own needs is a sin in the eyes of My Eternal Father.

So many false excuses, made in the name of self-worth, are completely unacceptable and against My teachings. Love one another. Treat others as you would expect to be treated yourself. Think of others needs before your own. Stand up for the human rights of your brothers and sisters when they face the injustice of others. Never ever justify punishing one person in order to gain material advantage. Show love and compassion even for your enemies. This is not an easy task because of the materialist insecurities My children feel. The symptoms of the selfish obsession with wealth, beauty and so-called success that many people believe to be natural attributes of the human make up cause terrible confusion.

The idea where people are brainwashed into putting their own needs first in the name of self-worth has been implanted in the human psyche for a long time but this philosophy has been reinforced by the powers of modern communication. When My children hear these messages almost daily through TV, the media, the cinema, music and the internet, they accept these messages as being important.

Despite the false promise, these beliefs, which are appealing in that they offer self-gratification, which is hard to reject, represent, My children accept the lie, the lie that has been planted by the Deceiver—Satan. The disquiet they feel soon afterwards, having taken advantage of someone else, is hard for them to understand. They, My children, having won the coveted prize are not happy. They then seek out more and more of the same, so insatiable is their appetite. But it is useless. They can't fully satisfy themselves. They are devoid of real joy, a natural contentment, and don't understand the emptiness they feel inside.

When you place yourself first before others, that is selfish. When you take unfair advantage over those who are weaker and more vulnerable than you, that is sinful. When you damage that person's ability to live in dignity and then deprive them of the right to feed their families adequately, that deeply offends Me. I suffer with these souls. Do onto your neighbor a wrong and you do this to Me. When you hurt your neighbor through words of spite you are guilty of inflicting pain in My heart.

When man punishes another through violence I endure the pain of My passion on the cross. I relive it. I feel their pain as you inflict bodily harm on them. When you are a murderer, you are guilty of the final indignity of nailing Me to the cross. Children know this. Sin will lead you to Hell. This is frightening for those believers who see Me as a merciful judge. My promise of unlimited mercy, which I will give to each and every one of you who repents, is still guaranteed. But how can I save those who will not see the error in their mixed up lives?

Preaching the truth of my teachings is important. It is because of the appeal of so many distractions which abound that many of My children will find it extremely difficult to recognize the word of God. Many will not have knowledge of God's teachings through the prophets or through Holy Scripture. Many simply don't want to know. For others they will refuse to listen even if the word is spread through My prophets and visionaries of today with clear signs for all to see. This is why it will be up to the believers to pray for the others. Special prayers are needed now. By praying to The Divine Mercy, the powerful prayer, given to My beloved Sister Faustina, much conversion will take place.

When that happens, I request that all My children rejoin in prayer groups to continue to pray for and give guidance to these prodigal children of Mine—your brothers and sisters. In My name and the Blessed Trinity, I urge My beloved children to join forces in union with My heart and help Me save their souls. I love them all so much that I weep sad and bitter tears of terror for them. I don't want to lose them.

Help Me, My followers in the light, to reunite these lost souls with My family so that they too will experience the true Paradise for which they strive so desperately. Hold out your hand to theirs. Talk to them. Listen to them. Show them compassion even when they throw it back in your face in scorn. Show patience. Above all, make them feel My love for them through you. They will find it hard to dismiss you then even if they mock you. Through your prayers you can, and will, save their souls.

I salute you My precious followers. You bring tears to My eyes with the love and devotion you show to Me, My Blessed Mother, Queen of the Heavens and the Blessed Trinity. We, and all the angels and saints in Heaven rejoice in your response to this calling now. So go do your work in the name of My Eternal Father. Bring back My flock.

Your devoted Savior, Jesus Christ. [xiii]

ALLOW ME TO BLESS YOU

I will give you hidden treasures, riches stored in secret places,
so that you may know that I am the LORD, the God of Israel,
who summons you by name..

(Isa. 45:3)

God's desire to bless and prosper us goes back to the time of Abraham: "Christ redeemed us in order that the blessings given to Abraham might come to us (Gentiles) through Christ Jesus, so that by faith we might receive the promise of the Spirit" (Gal. 3:13-14). But so far, we have tied God's blessings of prosperity to monetary value. God's prosperity goes beyond financial freedom and is meant to benefit others beyond yourself and your immediate family. The blessings of the Lord makes rich and adds no sorrow; and the wealth it brings according to the Scripture comes without painful toil. (Prov. 10:22). One may have all the financial wealth on earth, but without peace, joy, happiness, good health, and salvation, the wealth is incomplete. "For what good is it for someone to gain the whole world, yet forfeit their soul?" (Mark 8:36).

The prosperity of the Lord, even if late, comes with no strings, and it lasts. But wealth comes suddenly and with a price, and disappears as suddenly as it came if the source is not of divine will. When wealth comes according to the principles of divine laws, you sleep well at night, because the peace of God surrounds you and the love of God compels you to use your wealth for the good of all.

The truth is that we serve a God who rewards those who diligently serve Him. Let us take God at face value, believe His promises, and work with Him for a breakthrough that endures. Forget what we have learned about sowing seeds to receive from the Lord. While this is true and works; yet, there is more to it. God is looking for a relationship—call it a personal or marriage relationship, parent-child relationship, or whatever you want to name it. Just enter a relationship with God where you are comfortable talking to Him every day, like you would talk to someone whom you love, admire, trust, and respect. The heart of the giver is as much important as the giver's gift, according to the One who rewards all.

One day, as I was meditating on the Word of God, I perceived the Holy Spirit ministering in my spirit: Many of you say you know Me, have faith in Me, and love Me, but how can you say that you love Me and fail to keep my commandments? Did I not say in John 14:21 that "Whoever has my commands and keeps them is the one who loves me? The one who loves me will be loved by my Father, and I too will love them and show myself to them." And how can you say you trust Me but lack the faith to prove it, or say you have faith and worry so much about what you will eat, what you will wear, and what you will be?

Think about what the Lord is saying and approach Him for the grace if you feel He is speaking to you. It is a known fact that we live in a culture of materialism where everyone is in a hurry to get somewhere or make it at the expense of fairness, family values, moral decency, or whatever else stands in the way. How quickly we forget that all we need and chase after is in God's hands. After all, the earth is His fullness and everything in it (Psa. 34). And remember, "Seek first the Kingdom of

God and His righteousness and everything will be added onto you" (Matt. 6:33). 2 Corinthians 1:20 says: "No matter how many promises God has made, they are 'Yes' in Christ, and so through Him the 'Amen' is spoken by us to the glory of God." But when we rely so much on "who we know and what we know" and less on the divine principles and will, our "Amen" testifies to self and man, not God.

Some people would ask, what about the people who are making it without God in their lives? Indeed, the law of universal principles can allow anyone to make money and be successful without God, but it comes with a price. Some people toil and labor to make money while sacrificing family, moral values, and decency. Some make money by selling their souls to the devil. And some cheat, lie, blackmail, or use other people as a ladder to get on top. In any of these scenarios, success comes with inner emptiness, which is why so many rich people and celebrities are without peace, joy, and happiness.

Still ministering to me, I continued to write what I perceived the Holy Spirit is saying: My child, allow me to bless you and use you as an instrument of my blessings for others. Would you help Me? Would you, My child, be My arm with which I touch the hurting, the eye with which they see Me, and the voice with which I speak to your brothers and sisters? Will you help Me win souls? I am the bread of life and form the light and create darkness, I bring prosperity and create disaster; I, the LORD, do all these things (Isa. 45:7). I desire to give you financial freedom, but first, will you allow Me to give you the wealth of peace and joy, which is worth more than gold? I will bless you if you allow Me, My child.

What a Father, and what a generous invitation He extends to every one of us. Staying in the presence of God brings favor—a divine principle. Irrespective of whom you are, what you do, or whom you know or don't know, when God's favor rests upon you, you will be in your home and doors of breakthrough will open for you with limited effort. Psalm 127:2 says, "In vain you rise early and stay up late; toiling for food to eat—for He grants sleep to those he loves." The Lord blesses those who love him (Prov. 8:17). Maintaining a heart of gratitude and giving thanks in every situation is crucial to divine will and overflow. Those who do so have favor with God and man because they acknowledge that everything is from God, and encourage others, their giver with heart of gratitude.

If you spent as much time in the presence of God as you do running around town for promotion, banking double and triple overtime, networking, and jumping from one business idea to another, favor would come upon you and doors would be opened. Trust me on this! Remember how I told you about the glory of God coming down during a spirit-filled praise and worship session? Your worship calls down God's presence and the anointing that breaks every yoke. Anointing comes with favor, wisdom, and ideas of what can enrich you.

Prevailing in our generation is giving with the wrong intentions, motivated by vanity. Jesus wants us to present our needs and the needs of others with the right motives and attitudes (love, gratitude, humility, and with faith). I truly believe that when giving is motivated by love, it ignites mercy in time of need, help in trouble, and abundance in harvest time for you. The popular teaching of "believe it and claim it" is true for the most part; however, God looks at the heart and the intention of purpose when he releases prosperity into our hands. Seed sowing (giving and charity), one of the divine principles of prosperity is often misused when people are prompted to give out of self-interest that is motivated by vanity of the giver, or greed of the one who receives 'deceitfully'. I have nothing against giving of course; without which, I will not be where I am today. But let the truth be told for Scripture says: "let God be true and every man a liar; as it's written…" (Rm. 3:4).

Always speak to God about your seeds and let the Holy Spirit direct you. Never give to please anyone else but God. Yes, the Lord will always bless one who gives in sincerity and seeks wealth that glorifies Him. He knows the desires of our hearts and knows when we seek man's accolades out of vanity. God does not have time for selfish prayers, especially not now that He is looking for people to stand in the gap and help Him win souls before He comes again. This is my opinion by the way, but my guts tell me I am right on this. I will end by leaving you with another message, titled "Quest for Wealth," to show how unintended traps are set for those who devote all their attention in pursuit of wealth at any cost:

My beloved daughter, concentrate and listen to what I have to say. You are now in the throes of a transition from the time you received the first message to the present ones. Please understand that these messages are coming from Me and please stop your doubts now. This will enable you to concentrate on the work for which you have been called.

In relation to matters which are occurring in the world it is now becoming clearer by the day what the evil world order are trying to inflict on the world. The United Nations, one of the many fronts for this new world order, are trying to stamp out all My teachings and will use every lethal weapon at their disposal to do this. Fear not because My believers will fight hard and will not deny Me especially in those countries which are consecrated to Me and who have a devout and unshakable faith. They will not stand back and allow this. But for many because of the costs involved in ensuring that their children are guided in the light, they will be powerless. As explained to you before the wrath of My Eternal Father is about to be shown on the earth as man inches nearer and nearer in their attempts to disown Me.

The world looks the same. People seem the same. The world of television with its rose tinted appeal seems the same. People bury their heads in the sand. They think that the world will continue as it is. Sadly they are mistaken. My duty to My children is to save you. Not to allow you continue to be sucked into an empty vacuum of promises, empty dreams and false ambitions. These are the pleasures to which you gave allegiance for many, many years. These are the promises that those of you, through no fault of your own, were convinced was the path to follow for self-worth, Self-gain, Self-Reward. You were told to look after number one whatever the cost - the number one being you. You with your ambitions, lust for wealth for yourself and your children, desire to become better than your brothers and sisters, and a constant relentless quest for self-acclaim were fooled.

These ambitions were fed to My children, through the appeal and gloss of these ambitions by the Deceiver. Many of My children will laugh at this message and say that this is not true. Unfortunately the Deceiver exists and most of My children do not accept that he does. He is cunning in that he hides behind things, people, acts and appealing incentives. His glamorous allure means that, today, if you ask a person which they would accept—money or a chance to reunite with their lost families—and they will opt for money. Ask another if they would betray their brother or sister for material gain. And the answer will be yes. Ask a young child if they would trade their simple life for a life of wonder and excitement and the answer will be yes.

Why then do My children find it hard to understand that once the grand prize has been awarded to them do they then feel they need more and more? A wealthy man who gains once will constantly continue to attain more. The reason for this is that Satan's gifts leave a raw empty feeling inside you that you do not understand. So you continue in your quest to seek out more and it is usually at the expense of the welfare of your neighbor. No man gains huge wealth without the people he met on the way suffering to some degree. No person who gains fame will get there unless someone else has had to do without. A man that does not share his wealth is doomed. A person who has nothing tends to share more than those who have been blessed with material comforts.

My Teachings cannot be watered down. Why do My children ignore these teachings, taught by My apostles since the new scriptures were produced? Why do they not heed the doctrine they contain? Do they believe that they were written by My disciples so that people would not listen? These teachings have not changed since I left this earth. They are there for a reason. You can change their interpretation, water it down, add new meaning or delete some parts but one thing will remain. And that is the truth. The truth will always stay the same. It cannot and will not be changed to suit mankind. Heed this now. Sit up and listen. You cannot expect to follow this route and enter My Father's Kingdom. Many of you justify the wealth and glory you gain and attribute this to luck.

What you may not realize is that many of you sold your souls to the Evil One in the process. Some of My children do know that they have committed this grave sin and think nothing of it. Others genuinely believe that they are simply doing the best for themselves and their families but they must understand that financial security is acceptable. Quest for luxury and wealth is not. The reality is that vast amounts of wealth are gained through sin. Wealth that may be gained without sin will lead to sin.

Despite the teachings of My Father's Church throughout the world, people still do not accept My teachings. Wealthy people who strive for material gain have one God. Poor people who strive for wealth have one God. They are both the same. Money, money is useless if it is acquired dishonestly and where those less fortunate do not benefit from the experience. Money, material wealth and all good things gained by those people who consider themselves fortunate must be shared among those who need it. Money given away to charity is meaningless if it is done in order to seek glory or attention.

Be assured that with the evil that is being planned now in the world when the desire to leave you with empty pockets becomes a reality only then will you realize how little value money holds. When they, the evil entity, take over your money and render you powerless to touch it without agreeing to their terms then you will finally realize that you will need an alternative route to happiness.

Your money will be worthless. You will need then to survive the way of the jungle. Those with survival instincts will find it easier than those who never had to work on their bended knees before. Seeds to grow your own food will mean more to you than a million dollars. A simple fruit will mean more to you than a flashy car. Because when you are stripped bare you will call out to your maker, your creator. It is then, and only then, will you realize that all that matters is the love in your heart. Because without love you cannot grow, nor can you enter My Father's

Kingdom.

Think now. Be careful in your quest for wealth. Stop now before it is too late. Share and divide and follow My path. This is a tough lesson for My children who feel a sense of insecurity.

Your beloved Savior, Jesus Christ [xiv]

LIVE, LOVE AND WIN

Homes are built on the foundation of wisdom and understanding. Being wise is better than being strong; yes, knowledge is more important than strength.

(Prov. 24:3, 5)

This chapter lists some principal guidelines and knowledge that will encourage you to live, love, and win for yourself, your children, your spouse, and everyone. Like golden rules of fairness, there are more ways to love anyone and get along. Most of these guidelines are from notes taken on the night of my inspired lesson in love.[xv] Some of them are common-sense things that we ought to know. Some are probably things you have heard or read before, while others are simply Bible truths about how you must love unconditionally to win victoriously.

There is a popular saying that if you keep doing the same thing, you will keep getting the same result. I dare you to stop being predictable and step out of your old self and attitude into the new way to live, love, and win! Please note that while I have directed these bullet lists toward women, much of the advice also apply to all men who desire change to live, love and win.

WIN FOR YOU
- Love yourself with contentment by accepting who you are and remaining open to the Holy Spirit for directions.
- Stay compassionate, lovable, and teachable.

o Learn to be at peace with yourself and happy where you are.
o Laugh at your own foolishness and don't take everything personally.
o Don't think more highly of yourself than others; let humility exalt you.
o Be a prayerful woman, wife, and mother.
o Be a Proverbs 31 woman who holds her family together with inner beauty.
o Always make your home welcoming and not a war zone.
o Take an occasional time-out to rest, meditate, and exhale.
o Always remember you are the greatest asset of your family.

WIN WITH EVERYONE

o Accept the differences in people's personalities with respect.
o Expect and live with people's mistakes with patience, for you yourself are not perfect.
o Never rush to judgment and criticism.
o Avoid unrealistic expectations and keep an open mind.
o Never expect perfection or overnight change in anyone.
o Don't always strive to have it your way.
o Remember there are other ways to get things done for the same result.
o Don't be too demanding or bashful in your approach.
o Cut people some slack every once in a while.
o Give others the benefit of the doubt every so often.
o Learn to walk away from a heated argument before it leads to a fight.
o Offer forgiveness even when you don't think it is deserved.

o   Remember the good deeds a person did for you and don't dwell on past wrongs.

o   Always choose peace over simple irritation and arguments.

o   Choose kindness and consideration over being right.

o   Give and accept apologies freely.

o   Be appreciative of even little stuff.

o   Try not to take anyone for granted, for every child of God has value.

o   Do everything possible on your part to live in peace with others.

WIN WITH SPOUSE

o   Never try to change him forcefully with physical persuasion; let God do it.

o   See in him the love of God for you, for he is God's representative on earth for you.

o   Don't be dependent on him for total fulfillment; rather, pray that God uses him to fulfill His love for you always.

o   Love him as God's child unconditionally, for he is God's child before he became your spouse.

o   Never put him before God, but carry him along with faith in God alone.

o   Help him to become the leader that God asks him to be.

o   Respect his privacy, individualism, and differences.

o   Never be ashamed of him in public.

o   Never manipulate him through sex.

o   Learn to surrender him to God.

o   Pray for him and with him.

o   Always give thanks for him.

o   Know that he doesn't always have to agree with you or share your point of view in everything.

o   Avoid putting him down using derogatory words and remarks.

o   Fight the evil, negative thoughts and the nagging that come up whenever you see him.

o   Never go to bed angry.

o   Accept his faults with patience as Christ's cross for you.

o   Appreciate and recognize his strengths.

o   Praise and compliment him for what he does right.

o   Offer encouragement and suggestions in place of criticism whenever he makes mistakes.

o   Communicate your thoughts and feelings verbally and openly

o   Remember that he cannot read your mind—men don't just get it!

o   Laugh with him at his jokes and at his foolishness.

o   Give up stubbornness; be assertive, yet humbly in approach.

o   Cast away jealousy and start building trust for your marriage.

o   Listen more and think before you respond.

o   Avoid winning arguments for the sake of winning and starting fights for the sake of attention.

FOR YOUR CHILDREN

o   Be an encourager of your children; never demoralize.

o   Bless and never curse them, for there is power in your tongue.

o   Accept change as a fact of life.

o   Love your children, but never use them as weapon against a spouse.

o   Don't give your children everything they desire, for you may be setting them up for failure in the future.

o   Don't spare the rod and spoil the child; develop a way to discipline your children.

o   Bring up your children in the way of the Lord.

o   Pray the will of God for them, not your will.

o   Show and teach them by example - Don't fight, curse, cheat, be a drunkard, or promiscuous in front of your children.

o   Very important – follow through on the punishment threat for what your child would receive in defiance and disobedience; otherwise, they will call off your bluff the next time.

Finally, if you are ever disappointed, angry, or mad at anyone to the point of hatred, know that hatred is a spiritual weapon that can destroy you, and not just the person you hate. The power of love can evaporate hatred instantly, says the Lord in answer to the question of what to do when hatred comes upon you. This is a message given on August 26, 2012, titled "Hatred is the Cause of All Evil in the World and It Takes Many Forms." said the message read:

My dearly beloved daughter, hatred is the cause of all evil in the world and it takes many forms. Hostility towards another person springs from fear, the fear that this person may hurt you in some way. Disagreements with another person can come about because of the sin of pride. This is when you feel that you must prove your worth, at all costs, even if you are wrong. Jealousy very soon turns to hatred although it can be mild to begin with.

Dislike of oneself begins because you compare your life with others whom you feel have better fortune than you. Very soon this dislike develops into hatred of oneself and one's body. This then leads into sins of the flesh. Hatred may also develop because of the sin of coveting another's possessions. This can lead to war when one country covets the riches of another. Or it can mean allowing greed to consume your soul when you crave the same worldly riches as your neighbor. Envy also turns into a form of hatred especially when, no matter how hard you try to emulate another, you fail to achieve what you set out to do.

All sins, if allowed to fester, can lead you towards hatred. When you feel hatred, you must know that Satan has managed to invade your spirit. When this happens he will hold you in a vise-like grip and will not leave you alone. No matter how much you try to release his grip, he will hold onto you for dear life. Your only weapon is prayer. Pray, pray, pray when hatred surges through you. For until it leaves you, you can never feel peace, love or joy again. When hatred takes hold of your heart and soul, you become one step further removed from Me, your Jesus. You suffer terribly and feel anger and a helplessness which you cannot control. Never believe the final lie which Satan will plant in your soul, when he has cast a cloak of hatred over you.

The lie is this. Your hatred can only be dissipated when you seek final revenge on the target of your hatred. When you pray and ask me to help you, My answer will be this. Forgive your adversaries and those whom you believe are the cause of your hatred. But to forgive, you must humble yourself before Me and ask Me to forgive you first. Once you forgive those you hate you must then atone for your sin. Show your adversaries love. Fight hatred, a wicked and dangerous disease of the soul, with love. Love is the cure to rid your soul of this infestation. When you can do this, you would have defeated Satan and he will leave you be. Never be afraid to fight hatred in your soul even though you will find it very difficult. If hatred could be diluted in this way, through the humility of the sinner, peace would reign in the world. [xvi]

Your Jesus

INSPIRATIONS FOR DAILY LIVING

THE JOY OF SURRENDER AND HOW IT CAN BE ACHIEVED

Cast thy burden upon the LORD, and he shall sustain thee: he shall never suffer the righteous to be moved.

(Ps. 55:22)

During the latter part of my life's struggles and my journey to spiritual growth, I came to know more about God, who He is, and how to worship Him, but very little about how to surrender. I didn't know how because I thought that worshipping and trusting Him meant I had surrendered. This assumption is true for the most part, but not completely, because you can love and trust God faithfully and yet fail miserably when it comes to surrendering to Him. Because we are created for His purposes, we are called to surrender our lives, hopes, dreams, joys, sorrows, weaknesses, strengths, and struggles to His will, plans, and purposes.

The total surrender of one's daily life and issues is difficult for even the most trusting Christian. It is easy to say that you trust God, but resist His will when it's inconvenient or when you are afraid to hear what He has to say. Our inability to surrender lies in our human weaknesses, born of fear, selfishness, or lack of faith and instigated by the scheming of the devil, who intends to rob us of our inheritance. Once we doubt God subconsciously, we are holding Him to a limit and it becomes more difficult to surrender ourselves to His will.

To surrender is to submit completely to God's will for you and your family without reservation, even when it doesn't seem fair. Because we are created in His image and with the free will to worship Him out of pure love, it pleases God to reward those who freely choose Him and, choose good over evil. He knows our needs and can save us from any difficult situation, yet He does not jump in until we ask and surrender the situation to Him. He doesn't want to interfere, so He allows us to make our own decisions and be responsible for the outcomes.

Before I learned to surrender, I often felt like I was in control of everything and could rely on my own strength. I was often overwhelmed because I took on so much and let others dump so much on me. Then, one day, God revealed to me through the leader of the Isaiah Ministry[xvii] that while I trusted, I had not surrendered. This was the biggest shock and revelation of my life, because I knew and felt what she was talking about as soon as I understood the meaning of surrender.

I realized that I had come to rely so much on my own strength, abilities, and will power. So I learned and started praying for God's will. I began surrendering more issues to Him, and the events of my life took a different turn and meaning. I started feeling lighter as my baggage was lifted away. Oh, what a joy it is to surrender! I am talking specifically about the divine blessings and gifts of the Holy Spirit that brought peace, love, and joy into my heart and about the physical manifestations of blessings that followed.

The difference between trust and surrender is that with trust, you have confidence in God's ability to do all things because you believe. However, even though you believe, you are unable to give up control of those things out of fear that God may disappoint you or may not understand or do it fast enough. To surrender is to resign yourself completely to faith in God so that you can relinquish your issues, concerns, and loved ones to Him, knowing they are in good hands. For instance, you try to be a good parent to the children God entrusted into your care by doing your best, and then you surrender them by praying for them daily and let God worry about them, because you know He can take better care of them than you. Even if what you receive isn't what you expected, you submit in prayer ("let your will be done"), attitude -not worrying, and actions – by letting go, and trusting that the Lord is in control. Remember, His ways are not our ways and His thoughts not our thoughts (Isa. 55:8).

The act of surrendering is not achieved in a day, and certainly not through our own efforts, but by the grace that comes from the Lord. With me, it started when I gave up control and let God drive. I realized then that I didn't have to be the super problem-solver to be a hero. We have only one super problem-solver, the Alpha and Omega. He would not hesitate to take the burdens off our shoulders, if we would only let go and let Him. There have been times during my transformation process when I had become overwhelmed and let go of His hand out of fear, anxiety, impatience and self-reliance. I took on my issues onto my shoulders again. It has been a constant struggle to remain faithful in my submission, a battle fought and won by His grace.

Here is how to practice submission by praying for God's will: I seek God's opinion in prayers every day, on every issue and decisions as much as I can. I start by presenting what I think my options are and asking God in prayers what He thinks. (If I find peace and joy in the direction I plan to go, I know it is His will, else I am supposed to wait to get a release. But sometimes I am too impatient and that's where the trouble can start). If I am praying for something that I want, I ask to receive it only if that's His will for me, if it's not, I ask that I may find peace or have something else better in its place. If I am struggling with something or a situation, I pray that He mend the situation, soothe it or remove it completely from me, else let His will be done. After praying, I am usually able to live with the outcome in peace, knowing that He answered me either way.

In conclusion, surrendering is practicing humility, faith in God, obedience to his will, and bearing your cross patiently after Him. While I am still learning to hold onto Him faithfully as I walk, surrendering has given me assurance and confidence that cannot be shaken by any stress of this world. These feelings make me look forward to each day knowing that "nothing in His control would ever be out of control."

Surrendering is humility: When you humble yourself before God, He lifts you up. You must come to Him like a little child in total abandonment.

Surrendering is faith in God: Faith is believing in what you have not seen. If you know that He fulfills His promises, then you must wait on Him.

Surrendering is obedience to His will: Sometimes we can run, but we cannot hide. Without obedience, there is only so much we can achieve.

Surrendering is bearing afflictions and suffering with patience: We do this for the sake of Christ while waiting on Him. Any time we bear pain and insult for His sake, we're bearing His cross.

THE SECRET TO PRAYING EFFECTIVELY

*Ask, and you will receive; seek, and you will find; knock,
and the door will be opened to you. For everyone who asks
will receive, and anyone who seeks will find, and the
door will be opened to those who knock.*

(Matt. 7:7-8)

There is no weekend in the school of prayer; school is every day. If you want to pray better, you will have to pray more often, for praying better is a gift from God, but praying more is a personal choice. We often say we don't have time to pray because we are tied down with work. The problem, as the mother of God saw it, is not the schedule, but lack of love.[xviii] For when we love, we think less of ourselves. Through prayer we communicate and share intimacy with the Father. If we love, we will be able to pray more, not only for ourselves, but also for the world.

The more we pray, the more we open our hearts to the Holy Spirit to transform our love and the quality of our prayers and to intercede for us: "In the same way the Spirit also comes to help us, weak as we are. For we do not know how we ought to pray; the Spirit himself pleads with God for us in groans that words cannot express" (Rom. 8:26).

God our Father wants us to come to Him in prayer with our needs at all times. Turn to Him and seek His will in your daily life and in every decision. When you do, whatever you ask with faith and in thanksgiving will be received if you believe (Matt. 21:22). For everything in life, prayer is the answer: "Be joyful always, pray at all times" (Thes.5:16-17). Approach Him with your problem so He can solve it, with your petitions so He can grant them, with your confusion so He can unravel it, and with your spouse so He can change him.

However, God is not a robot to be toyed with and dropped at our leisure, nor a messenger to be commanded and exploited only for our needs. He wants a real relationship with us. Because of the Blood of the Lamb that has atoned for our sins, He desires a "father/child" relationship with us, not a "master/servant" relationship. He wants a relationship communicated in prayers through praises, exultation, and repentance while bringing petitions and thanksgiving to the Father through the Son, Jesus.

So before you present your petitions, acknowledge Him with praises, for He is worthy of all praises. Exult and flatter the Lord; adore, magnify, and worship Him for His glory and majesty. Present your needs with gratitude and thanksgiving for the gifts and blessings already received. Recognize your sinfulness before Him and ask for forgiveness with sincerity. "He forgives our sin, not because of who we are, but for his sake" (Isa. 43:25). Finally, surrender to Him your weaknesses; He knows about them and can work with anything if only you are willing.

He is always waiting inside for that knock, so He can open the door. Until we knock, we are choosing to go through life's struggles alone. God hurts with us when we hurt, but He cannot do much to console us until we run to Him for shelter and safety. God wants us to rely on Him as a Father and our God, not on ourselves or on other people or things. Our Lord is a jealous God (Deut. 4:24) and does not like to share His glory with anyone.

There are different types of prayer. Most people pray the traditional way by speaking to God with words from the heart. Others pray with spiritual songs, psalms, and hymns. Those who worship with hymns and songs pray twice, for they are pleasing sounds to the Lord. Then there is silent and contemplative prayer—you go to God in prayer just by being silent in His presence, meditating on His words, and contemplating His creation, mystery, and passion on the cross. Practicing this type of prayer allows you to hear from Him quicker because the Holy Spirit speaks to us when we are silent enough to hear. No matter how you choose to communicate with God, do it from your heart and soul; avoid distractions, because God is a spirit and we must communicate with Him in spirit.

Prayer is the only way for us to overcome our weaknesses and receive help. Through prayer, we surrender to change and to the will of God. Through prayer, we admit that we cannot do it on our own, and gradually, the Holy Spirit will take over and turn things around. By praying at every opportunity, we open up our hearts to God. There is no best or set time to pray; however, set a time and schedule if it helps you to become more faithful. Pray any time—when you wake up, at bedtime, during the day, while driving, during meals, when experiencing setbacks, at work, at home, and so on.

There will be times when you don't feel like praying anymore because you are tired, and you feel that your prayers are not being answered. When this happens, don't despair, but pray even more for the gift of perseverance. Get on your knees and pray for the grace to continue to pray. When you try to please God but fail, don't worry or get discouraged; He understands our desires, strengths, and weaknesses. He will help you to become faithful if your desires are sincere.

Often, our prayers are selfish in nature. All we do is ask God to fulfill our needs, and we forget to give thanks for answered prayers and little favors; we pray for ourselves and our immediate families, but nobody else. God calls us to intercede for each other, believers and unbelievers alike. Pray for the world that is constantly sinning against Him, so we may obtain peace, God's mercy, and pardon. (By the way, praying for a spouse or someone else who is hurting you is the fastest way to bring them to repentance, and praying for someone whom you have difficulty forgiving is the quickest way to achieve forgiveness.)

As you learn to pray effectively, I urge you to answer the call to pray more so that the Holy Spirit will lead you to His love and His will for you. When this happens, your heart becomes receptive to change, and this opens up many more possibilities. When you do, you'll begin to feel the healing transformation within as you empty yourself out to the control of the Holy Spirit.

In conclusion, you will see improvements in the quality of your prayer life if you pray more often. You will pray better:

- By choosing to pray more even when you are discouraged.

- By building a relationship with God.

- By giving praise and thanksgiving when you pray.

- By showing repentance and contrition before God.

- By forgiving your transgressors so that your prayers will not be hindered.

- By interceding for others.

- By worshiping Him in spirit and in the sincerity of your heart.

- By being still in His presence and listening to Him.

- By meditating and contemplating His mysteries and passion.

- By praying for His will in your life always.

Finally, when it comes to prayer, many people often wonder what form and method of prayer is preferred. Our Lord in one of the messages to MDM explained how simple a prayer can be. He said, and I quote from his message of April 30th, 2012:

[xix]"**Prayer means to ask. Prayer means to communicate. Prayer means to show love and give thanks.** Many people today, well-meaning and of generous heart do not know how to pray. Some will find it distasteful and will feel awkward. Others will feel that their prayers won't count. Oh how I love these special souls. So far removed and yet how I yearn to show them My deep love.

I call on all of you who don't know Me. There is no need to fear Me. All you have to do is to ask Me to take you and give you comfort. Let Me prove My love. Speak to Me in your own simple words. Nothing will shock Me. Confide in Me your worries as I will soothe your heart. Let Me help you to feel true peace. Ask Me to sort out your concerns. I will show you the truth so that your worries will no longer seem as bad.

How will you know I hear you? How will you be sure that I will respond to you? Just sit down quietly and ask Me to help you with this prayer to help you open your heart to Me and to ask for My help. Many of you will not come to Me at this time. But that is okay. In times of hardship, confusion and fear you will. I stand with you every day although you do not realize this yet. But very soon you will see Me and know the truth of My promise to grant you eternal life in Body, Mind and Spirit."

Your Jesus

ESSENTIALS OF LIVING HAPPIER

Having therefore these promises, dearly beloved,
let us cleanse ourselves from all filthiness of the flesh
and spirit, perfecting holiness in the fear of God.

(2 Cor. 7:1)

You can achieve fame and acquire all the wealth in the world and yet not be happy. You may find happiness and contentment at some point; however, any fulfillment outside of God is temporary, which means that a man's inner mind won't rest until it rest fully in God. Living happier is living the abundant life promised to us through faith in Christ and obedience to His will. God said that if we choose Him, we choose life, but we choose death when we reject and disobey Him (Deut. 28:1-8). He promised to reward us with prosperity, fertility, good health, and much more when we choose obedience, as in Deuteronomy 28.

Money, fame, and fortune bring pleasure, no doubt, yet you cannot buy happiness. We are happier when we try to please God by the lifestyle we choose, even though it doesn't seem that way sometimes. God called every- one to a lifestyle of holiness (love of God and man): "Follow peace with all men, and holiness, without which no man shall see the Lord" (Heb. 12:14). It is a fact that a man finds "lasting" happiness and peace not by the size of his pocket, but by the choices he makes out of fear of the Lord and the lifestyle he chooses. Remember, we are tested by the events and circumstance of our life, and every heart that remains steadfast to the end will be rewarded.

Everyone's idea of happiness varies. To many, it's all about material wealth and possessions: the mansion we live in, the car we drive, the expensive clothes we wear, et cetera. While these are all good, materialism can create serious emptiness in life unless it is used wisely with the essential ingredients for happier living. If you have those, your joy will be complete, inside and out. I'm talking about simple things that money can't buy. A person who has little money, but more of these essentials, will live happier than one who has everything, but lacks the essential ingredients.

There are many more ingredients to happiness, but this book only touches on six:

1. **Living in holiness (obedience, peace, and love).** Living in holiness is the quickest and surest way to happiness. Holiness is not meant for the saints alone. Holiness is to love God with all your heart and your neighbor as yourself. Holiness is the fear of the Lord that enables us to practice humility, integrity, patience, love, forgiveness, charity, purity, obedience, and all the good virtues. It empowers and enriches our lives because of the rewards and the blessings that come to those who practice it. For instance, you will be a much happier person living in peace with yourself, your neighbor, and your environment.

2. **Living in simplicity and modesty.** Simplicity is not living in poverty, but rather living within your means; not frivolous but wisely, and giving thanks always for the much or little you have. There are people who live above their means with high credit card debts, high mortgages, high car notes, and expensive tastes

and habits. Such people deceive themselves into thinking they can afford to live this way because their paychecks meet the minimum payment. They compete with everyone to have more things and end up missing the best years of their lives in worries, stress, and sicknesses that could have been avoided. Their lives become a daily struggle because of high obligations, which affects the qualities of family relationships, health, and peace of mind. How can you be at peace knowing that there is only a thin line between you and homelessness if you lose your paycheck? And, live happy if you are always stressed out, thinking about the bills and hiding from the collectors? My simple advice; think about simplifying your life and living habits if you stand to lose everything within 1-3 months of losing your job or business income.

3. **Living like a child (at heart)**. A child surrenders to a parent, trusting that dad and mom know what is best. Relax your mind and attitude and lean on God like a child. Please remember that life is for the living, not the dead. Don't get bogged down seeking perfection, and missing the point. Life is not that uptight if you know the promise we've received. Children have issues, but they forget easily; they fight, but they forgive easily; they are afraid, but they trust easily. They do not discriminate, and they learn to obey parents. Christ said, "Verily I say unto you, whosoever shall not receive the kingdom of God as a little child shall in no wise enter therein" (Luke 18:17).

4. **Practicing forgiveness**. Many people weighed themselves down with grudges for years and not realized it. Remember, it is dangerous not to forgive, because it keeps you down and keeps your prayers from being answered. Forgive people, and forgive yourself, in order to be freed from the weight of anger, hatred,

and bitterness that comes with holding grudges. If you want to feel lighter today, try letting go of past hurts. Forgive that old friend or family member who has been difficult. Give that person a call; I bet he or she will be glad to hear from you. Forgiving your transgressors, asking to be forgiven from those you've wronged, and confessing your sin to free your heart from guilt is essential to living happier.

5. **Living in contentment**. Just like simplicity, contentment is being happy with what you have today by showing appreciation to the giver. The fact that you do not have enough today doesn't mean you can't have a lot tomorrow— but first you will have to be faithful and grateful for the little you have. Contentment helps to guard against being greed, as well as envy and jealousy of what others have. It stops you from misplacing your priorities and struggling for things that aren't really important: St. Paul said: "Make it your aim to live a quiet life, to mind your own business, and to earn your own living, just as we told you before. In this way you will win the respect of those who are not believers, and you will not have to depend on anyone for what you need" (Phil. 4:11-12). No matter where you are today, remember that you are still better off than a lot of people. Believe me, if you ever feel low or depressed; go volunteer your time to the less fortunate. See if that doesn't make you feel lucky enough to count your blessings.

6. **Living in the glory of God (exultations)**. Praising God lifts up our spirits to unite with the heavenly host, dissolving our inner sorrow and replacing it with joy, peace, and tranquility. Acknowledging God's presence with praise, especially when you are feeling down and lonely, is comforting and uplifting.

Praise Him when you are rejoicing and when you are hurting. Praise Him even when you don't understand anything anymore, and you don't feel like praising Him. Most importantly, praise Him in every situation, for that is God's will for you (1 Thess. 5:18). The power of the Holy Spirit melts away the tears and break down the walls of Jericho in your life as you do. Trust God with praise, and worship Him with thanks, for he is faithful to those who exalt him. Then experience for yourself the amazing power of praise when you sing and dance unto the Lord. Above all, Praises break yokes and set captives free.

In summary, we will be happier if we do our best to follow the gospel truths, study the word of God, and practice what it teaches as much as possible. The good news is that God does not expect us to do it on our own. Changing your attitude and practicing living for today, instead of worrying about tomorrow (Matt. 18) will bring you so much joy, peace, and happiness! Then, trust that God will bless you and bring you to the level where he wants you to be, for the Lord provides for those He loves while they are asleep (Psalm 127: 2). [Hint: Don't live for change. Change to live!] A friend of mine testified to me that her spouse started to change for good after he noticed the changes in her and how happier she has been of late. She told me that all she did was to start putting some of these ideas into practice to live happier, and felt the weight lifted off her shoulders.

Summary of Living Happier

- It is living in holiness, obedience, and love.

- It is living in praise and gratitude to God.

- It is living in simplicity; not above your means.

- It is total abandonment and reliance on God, like a child.

- It is abandoning those things that stress you out.

- It is abandoning those things that separate us from the love of God.

- It is about giving your time and money to charity

- It is about a change of attitude and getting rid of old baggage.

- It is about not sweating the small stuff.

- It is living in peace with yourself and your environment.

- It is letting go of past hurts through forgiveness.

- It is living with gratitude and humility, whether rich or poor.

- It means living for today and not worrying about tomorrow.

ACHIEVING FORGIVENESS THE EASIER WAY

Then Peter came and said to Him,
"Lord, how often shall my brother sin against me
and I forgive him? Up to seven times?"

(Matt. 18:21)

We all struggle with forgiveness, especially when it involves someone who has caused us pain, grief, and anguish. It is annoying to have to forgive someone who has tested your endurance by disappointing you over and over, and upsetting when the betrayal comes from someone close to home. But you know what? Where there is a will, there is a way. You can learn to forgive if you desire it enough, because God will give you the grace. It takes His grace to forgive as often as we are called to forgive.

We struggle especially to forgive a person, who has shown no remorse, and would probably throw it back in your face and cause you more pain by denying all wrongdoing in the first place. The most difficult thing is summoning up the courage to call this person who is probably going to view your olive branch as an admission of wrongdoing on *your* part. Besides these worries, the major hindrance to forgiveness is pride. Despite all the valid reasons, please, do not be deterred anymore, for it is definitely worth the cost.

Forgiveness is like a therapy prescribed by God. Forgiveness is to the soul what Advil is to a headache and migraine. We offer forgiveness to our transgressors, not only so that we too may be forgiven, but also for the healing of mind and soul. When you forgive, you free yourself from the weight of bitterness. When you forgive, you are offering the pain and disappointment to God in exchange of freedom and forgiveness of your own sins. Un-forgiveness and grudges, on the other hand, open up the devil's playground. That is why most unforgiving people exhibit signs of strong animosity, bitterness, and anguish - qualities that are harmful to the body and soul. If you cannot offer forgiveness for the sake of the person who offended you, offer it for yourself, please.

I have often thought I would never be able to forgive certain individuals because of how I felt. I was reluctant to forgive and even if I managed to, I didn't want to forget. But you know what? Anything is possible when there is a will. Not only have I been able to forgive, I have forgotten as well. I feel no remorse, animosity, anger, anguish, or bitterness towards anyone. I will have to admit, there are still a few that I struggle with when I remember, but I will never stop trying until I forgive and forget through the grace of God. You'll understand as I share my views and secrets to encourage you in your own struggles to forgive.

Praying for someone who has offended us is an easy way to achieve forgiveness. When you pray for the person, the temptation to hate will be suppressed. The Holy Spirit will lift off the burden and help you to forgive. Stop worrying about how to forgive an offender who betrayed your friendship without exposing yourself to the same situation in the future. The important thing is making the effort to forgive the person in your heart. Refuse to entertain any bitter thoughts against him or her. Making contact or resuming friendship should be secondary.

Forgiveness is not dependent on friendship. Don't hold off forgiveness because you are not ready to speak to the person yet. I used to be concerned and confused about forgiveness and friendship. For instance, when I no longer want to have anything to do with a person who betrayed my friendship and trust, I would be reluctant to offer forgiveness in order to avoid any contact with the person. As a Catholic, I spoke to a priest about my concerns, because I felt it was hypocritical to forgive when I am reluctant to speak to the person again, talk less of continuing the friendship. He made it clear that I can forgive without renewing the friendship, as long as I bear no grudge or animosity in my heart. Always choose to forgive and release your offender from the bitterness of heart; and the rest will take care of itself when you are ready.

Besides, God expects us to live in peace with each other, but He did not mandate that we *must* all be close friends. In fact, the Bible says that if your left eye is causing you to sin, it is better for you to cut it out than to have two eyes land you in hell (Matt. 18:19). In other words, if a particular person is keeping you from offering forgiveness, it is better to avoid the person by cutting off the friendship than to keep fighting and holding grudges. However, you should not hold malice against any one such as refusing to acknowledge or share pleasantly ("hi, hi") when you meet.

Making contact is ideal, but forgiveness starts from the heart and extends outward. The only way I was able to forgive certain individuals was by limiting the friendship and contact. My willingness to let go and initiate forgiveness in my heart without holding grudges or animosity towards anyone was my Christian way of starting the forgiving and healing process. The rest is up to the Holy Spirit. You must be sincere in your desire to forgive. If you are not sincere in your desires to let go of all resentment, you will be struggling for nothing. God sees our hearts and crowns our efforts.

Regarding "Forgiving and Forgetting", sometimes I understand that it is very hard to act like something never happened, but as a Christian, why forgive if you do not want to forget? To me, forgetting is the final phase of being freed. If I am not able to do that, then I am allowing myself to become the victim all over. Think about it; the person who hurt you may have moved on a long time ago, but you're left with a distasteful and bitter feeling whenever you remember. I don't think it's fair, yet if Christ can help me forgive, He can help me forget also if I ask.

Forgiveness does not come easily to any of us but I personally don't want to miss out on all the good things God is offering me by holding on to the things of the past. Remember, if we find reasons not to forgive others and forget; God could find many reasons not to forgive us as well. The Scripture says that He forgives us as often as we ask and remembers not: "It is I, who wipe out, for my own sake, your offenses; your sins I remember no more" (Isa. 43:25). What about people who offended you by mistake; should you not offer forgiveness freely as you have been forgiven? To err is human; to forgive is divine.

The ease of forgiveness normally depends on who the offender is and the degree of the offense. You have the "repeat" offenders, who are like temptations planted by the devil to test your endurance. This category of offenders may gossip about you, lie about you, and take advantage of your willingness to forgive. Gossipers are slanderers who lack something in themselves and need your prayers for their repentance. I suggest ignoring them and forgiving, even those who dislike you for just being yourself and no other reason, for they know not what they are doing anyhow.

Remember, everyone cannot like you, especially if you are in the ways of the Lord. Besides, it does you no good to get wrapped up in the web of someone who doesn't understand the spiritual implications of this sin. God is very clear about judgment for those who gossip and carry vicious rumors that destroy other people's homes and happiness.

The next category includes the people in your path who are purely selfish, proud, or stubborn. They are clueless as to how they affect other people around them because they're consumed with themselves. They refuse to get off their "high horses" and understand that life is not all about them. It is harder for such a person to show remorse or to admit any wrongdoing, making them the hardest to forgive. My advice to you is not to let anyone, and even them to hold you to un-forgiveness. God has asked us to forgive everyone so that He will in turn forgive us. It is our agreement with God and He would have to hold us to this agreement.

Entrust everything to God. Do your best to let go of past pain and bitterness, and start living freely again. Jesus answered Peter how many times we are supposed to forgive: "No, not seven times, answered Jesus, but seventy times seven" (Matt. 18:22). Forgive each time, and release the person to the Holy Spirit to convict. The worst thing you can do to yourself is to be vengeful. God is equally clear in Roman 12:19 that vengeance is His: "Forgive and do not return insult for insult, nor be revengeful, for vengeance is mine, says the Lord".

You know what else is soothing? Being the bigger person and initiating forgiveness by asking for it from someone that you have offended. Sometimes we know we've done something wrong, but pride often keeps us from asking for forgiveness. If you find it hard to ask to be forgiven, do you think it's easier on anyone else to ask for your forgiveness? Think about it! Jesus said that forgiveness is the pathway to freedom in his message of May 21st, 2011 to MDM and I quote:

"My daughter forgiveness is the pathway to freedom. When you forgive those who offend you or who have caused you hurt you become free of spirit. That is when joy fills your soul. That too means that I am present within you. When you forgive others this is a sign of love, not only for your neighbor, but love for Me your Divine Savior. For those who do not believe Me know that when they, too, forgive others I am present and walk with them. Yet they have no idea that this is the case.

Forgiveness is love. My love is endless. But I implore you, My children, to allow Me to forgive you for your sins. If you could only ask Me, to do this not only will you be free but the love and the joy you will experience will surprise you. This act of humility will allow you to communicate with love towards others. Your light will shine and will affect others in a special way but neither you nor they will be aware of this. My love, after the act of Redemption takes place, will flood your soul. Your clean soul will be like a magnet as it draws others towards you.

To forgive others is not easy My children. Pride and a sense of self-worth prevent this great act of mercy taking place. This is the work of Satan; for he knows that lack of forgiveness leads to other more serious sins against God the Father. When you cannot forgive others first of all, it builds up a resentment which, when it festers, leads to hatred and even murder. In many cases it can lead to war.

If people everywhere forgave one another graciously then hatred would not exist. Murder would be less frequent and love, the love of God, The Eternal Father, would spread. Learn to forgive one another. Push pride aside and ask for My Mercy. For when you ask for something according to My Holy Will you will be granted your request."

Your Jesus

THE BLESSING OF SEEING GOD IN OTHERS

*There is no need to write you about love for each
other. You yourselves have been taught by
God how you should love one another.*

(1 Thess. 4:9)

There is beauty and purpose in all God's creation. He created us equal
and loves everyone the same. We are made in the image and likeness of
God (Gen. 1:27) and each of us has a special gift and uniqueness in life.
For this reason, no one should be made to feel inferior by us based on
race, class, creed, or financial status. Christ instructs us to see Him in
the face of others when we show love: "Truly I tell you, whatever you
did for one of the least of these brothers and sisters of mine, you did
for me." (Matt. 25:40). It means seeing the beauty in every soul and
loving selflessly: "Since you are God's dear children, your life must be
controlled by love, just as Christ loved us and gave his life for us"
(Eph. 5:1-2).

Seeing God in others helps us to show compassion, kindness,
patience, charity, hospitality, and forgiveness. By so doing, we are
fulfilling the call to love:

> "I may be able to speak the languages of human beings and
> even of angels, but if I have no love, my speech is no more
> than a noisy gong or a clanging bell. I may have the gift of
> inspired preaching; I may have all knowledge and understand

101

all secrets; I may have all the faith needed to move mountains—but if I have no love, I am nothing. I may give away everything I have, and even give up but if I have no love, this does me no good". (1 Cor. 13:1-3)

Unfortunately, human beings tend to love selfishly and for the wrong reasons. We love people who love us first; those we are attracted to, and anyone you look up to who can contribute value to your life. Seeing God in others empowers us to love indiscriminately and it comes with a reward. Just as God comfort us in our distress, we too must comfort others who are in distress when we recognized Christ's sufferings in every face in distressed. St. Paul wrote: "We urge you, our friends, to warn the idle, encourage the timid, help the weak, and be patient with everyone. See that no one pays back wrong for wrong, but at all times make it your aim to do good to one another and to all people" (1 Thess. 5:14-15).

The fact that two people are different does not make one better than the other. It is what makes us unique that makes us who we are. Accept each individual's unique differences as strengths, not weaknesses or faults. It is not very noble to feel superior to others simply because of affluence—remember it is the Lord who gives: "For everyone who exalts himself will be humbled, and he who humbles himself will be exalted" (Luke 14:11). Treat everyone with respect and see the value in all people regardless of their importance in society, so that others may see God through you. "This is what we are called to do, to be the light to the world" (Matt. 5:14) and a reflection of Christ for everyone to see.

The blessings of seeing God in others is abundant and beyond measure. It is refreshing to know that the Lord loves and protects those who treat others fairly and forgives sin because of charity and almsgiving. Christ would also say to you, "Come here, my faithful child:

I was hungry and you fed me, thirsty and you gave me drink, I was a stranger and you welcomed me in your homes, naked you clothed me; I was sick and in prison you took care of me" (Matt. 25: 42-43).

Unfortunately, there are people who have the inclination to hate instantly. The truth is that we tend to dislike those different from us, those we cannot understand, and even those we secretly wish to be like. When you take a closer look at any individual, you will surely find something beautiful and unique, in that soul—perhaps the free spirit! For instance, if you dislike the way your co-worker talks, what about the way he responds to people's needs in the office? Judging others hinders us from recognizing the good in them. God does not see and judge the way the world does. In the Sermon on the Mount, Jesus taught that the poor in spirit, the gentle, the merciful, the pure in heart, and the peacemakers are blessed (Matt. 5:3-12).

This sermon, in its full context, says a lot about how God views self-worth and how we should view it. He determines our worth, not by our appearance and achievements, but by what's on the inside. The call to live the message of love can be achieved through peace: peace among men (love), peace between man and God (obedience), and peace within man (knowledge of God Word). Love is the key. Jesus said in his messages of March 14, 2012 that the blessing of seeing God in others is a gift given by grace to help us love and defeat the power of hatred in all its forms. Jesus is the light that creates this spontaneous love which brings souls together, therefore in Him, we are able to love God and all men. In the message[xx], He has this to say about love and how to receive the gift:

> "You can only show real love to others when you love Me. It is through love that you will be blessed with the gifts of looking at other human beings through My heart which is full of love and compassion. It is only when you show Me true love that your life

will change and joy will surge through your daily life. Never fear My love children. It is there for you all in abundance if you could only turn to Me and ask for it. Once you receive this love be generous with it. Spread My love everywhere so that all of you, especially lukewarm souls, can invite Me into their souls. This is the only way to salvation"

Furthermore, Love is more powerful than hatred. Continuing in the words of the message ((March 14, 2012), Jesus called us to conquer hatred with love. I quote:

> "Love is more powerful than hatred. Hatred is diluted if it is responded to with love. If someone treats you unjustly you must respond with love and satan will cower in pain. If you feel tempted to seek revenge on those who hurt you then you must pray for them, forgive them and show them love instead. Love, which permeates through My family on earth, is a very powerful force. You must never believe, for one instant, that hatred can defeat love. The power that hatred wields, although ugly and painful to witness, can be defeated through the power of love. How can love weaken hatred in the world today? Prayer is the answer.
>
> Love Me. Listen to Me. Respond to the requests of My beloved Mother and Me, her Son, through the various prayers given to you. I love you children.
>
> You must never feel disheartened when you see the wickedness around you. Your prayers can dilute this wickedness. Your love will defeat it. Your loving Savior, Jesus Christ"

In summary, here are few basic points to reflect on as a guide. Love one another as Christ has commanded and be a light for others to see by your words and actions, that you may possess your inheritance:

- Remember there is a purpose for everyone's existence. Let patience and humility guide you always.

- Let the understanding of human differences keep you compassionate. Never discriminate in your treatment of others.

- Never dwell on weaknesses; rather, recognize the other's strengths.

- Don't be conceited or presumptuous. Never judge someone simply because of another's perception.

- Fight the negative thoughts that come when you are around people you don't like.

- See everyone's uniqueness and worth.

- Accept people for who they are, not who you expect them to be. Imagine the face of God in every face you meet.

- When necessary, place yourself in other people's shoes.

- Treat others the way you would want to be treated.

- Show love by example through kind words and deeds.

- Never expect everyone to be like you and to achieve what you have achieved.

- Never expect everyone to agree with you.

- Extend helping hands and offer encouragement and suggestions when needed.

- Lower your expectations to avoid being easily disappointed.

- Give compliments and recognition to the deserving.

- Never stereotype or judge people because of their race, color or creed.

- Do not irritate others to the point of discouragement.

- Always do what you can to live in peace with others.

MY LOVE LETTER TO GOD

This is the love letter I wrote to God on the day I had the intriguing conversation that changed my life forever. I considered the experience a conversation with God because I found myself asking a lot of questions in my defense and His answers to every question came to me as quickly as I asked. The reason that I am publishing this letter is first to glorify God. I also want to show my state of mind during that encounter, even though I wasn't sure what I was writing then, as I went from despair to joy by the end of it all. I hope it will inspire others who love God to communicate with Him in writing, as well as in spirit, because He awaits your letter either way. This letter was written in 2002 on the night of my lesson in love.

Dear Lord, I love you because you loved me first. Father, I love you because you have been patient with me, loving and blessing me with life, health, and prosperity while waiting on me to return back to you. Jesus, I love you even more now because I have come to realize and appreciate what your death meant for me and for the world. I am so touched by your selfless love, so touched by our Father's generosity in sending you to us, so touched by your humility in taking it all, and submitting, even into death when you didn't have to. Lord Jesus, how unappreciative the world has been for your most bitter passion and pain. I love you, Jesus, and desire to love you even more for giving me the greatest joy and blessings such as renewing my personal relationship with you.

As I write this, Lord, I'm engulfed by emotion because I realize how incapable I am of loving you. My human weakness and fallen nature are limiting my full capability to love as much as I desire. Yet, I thank you, Jesus, for your strength is made manifest in my weakness and your grace is sufficient for me. When my sisters asked me about my intended pilgrimage to Medjugorje, my thoughts were that the good Lord would make it happen even though I did not have the means to go then. My faith and trust are what kept me going. Holy Trinity, I thank you because lately I have found new strength, peace, and joy in you. I have complete confidence that you have heard and answered all my prayers, answers which will be manifest at the appointed time.

I have equally come to appreciate more the depth of your love, faithfulness, and loyalty in calling us all to repentance and conversion to be saved, instead of abandoning us to perish in our sinful and shameless ways. As I meditate on the passion of Christ, your agonizing heart and tears on the cross, including the tears and sorrows of your mother Mary, I pray that your death will not be in vain for your world, and for the triumph of the immaculate heart of your mother, Mary. As you are willing to save me, Jesus, by your death, I know you would be even more willing to give me everything else to make me happy serving you. You said to seek first your kingdom and everything else will be added onto me. Your face, Lord, do I seek. I must confess that I am still not a good listener. Please give me discernment to understand when you speak to me, Lord. Teach me how to listen so that we will have perfect communication.

Whenever I visit you in the Blessed Sacrament Tabernacle, I feel you standing next to me and watching over me. I am filled with your presence as I spend quiet and quality time with you. You are truly my Emmanuel, God with me. Your presence overshadows me and gives me comfort and peace. When I am troubled and sob to you in prayer, you always comfort me and the peace that comes over me is what confirms your presence.

Thank you, God, the Father; God, the Son; and God, the Holy Spirit; Holy Trinity, I adore you. Thank you, blessed Mother of God and all the heavenly hosts who stay with us during adoration, praying with us and for us. When I think of what I am doing now in the early hours of the morning, writing and conversing with the Spirit, I smile and give praises that you have worked so mysteriously in my life.

I thank you, Father, and love You, and ask that Your will be done in my life always, Amen.

[This portion of the book can be reprinted, in part or in full, for any use. I ask God to bless anyone who reads this letter to glorify the Lord.]

THE WARNING - WHAT IF?

Many people are beginning to notice that the world we know is changing rapidly. Many have felt in their spirits that something is definitely wrong, but can't figure out what and why. Many are clueless or just don't care. And a lot more people agree that we are nearing the end time. While this book is not about the Second Coming message, I found it relevant to support the need for people to reevaluate their lives at this time and not focus their energy on worldly gain alone.

The compelling reason for shifting focus from materialism to spiritual gain now more than ever is the fact that spiritual gain leads to eternal life as well as fulfills our physical needs, including inner peace and joy which money cannot buy. The other strong reason to start thinking about spiritual and eternal life at this point is the possibilities of "what if?"

What if it is true that Christ is coming back soon, as He said He would? What if this is the era? What if the Second Coming warning messages contained in *The Book of Truth* are true? What if the past and current prophets and visionaries are not lying? What if the signs of disorder in the world today are only the beginning of the end? What if the end is here—what are you going to do? Are you ready? Think about it. What if…?

I am compelled by my spirit to make everyone that crosses my path aware of the warnings of the end-time prophecies and let you decide for yourself. The reason for the warnings and messages is that God is ever merciful and wants to give people a chance to repent so they can enter the new Paradise. The messages are being revealed to the world quickly because, according to Maria Divine Mercy, "we don't have much time before these events unfold in the world and people have a right to know the truth so they can examine their lives in the hope that their souls can be saved."

THE WARNING

New prophecies received by European Visionary reveal global events in the lead up to the Second Coming

WHY IS THE WARNING TAKING PLACE?

- To prove to all that God exists.

- To bring everyone back to Jesus and the way of the truth.

- To dilute the impact of sin and evil in the world through conversion.

- To help save us before the final day of judgment by giving us a chance to ask for forgiveness for the sins we have committed.

- To convert non-believers who would have no chance of redemption without this great act of mercy.

- To strengthen the faith of believers.

WHAT WILL HAPPEN DURING THE WARNING

- Every one over the age of 7 will experience a private mystical encounter with Jesus Christ which will last anything up to 15 minutes

- It is a gift from God the Father to convert people back to the truth. It is how the Final Day of Judgment will unfold only this time you will not be condemned. Instead you will be given a chance to ask for forgiveness.

- Two comets will collide in the sky.

- People will believe it to be catastrophic worse than an earthquake But it is not – it is a sign that Jesus has come.

- The sky will turn red it will look like a fire & then you will see a large cross in the sky to prepare you first.

- Atheists will say it was a global illusion. Scientists will look for a logical explanation but there won't be one.

- It will be spectacular and will not hurt us because it comes as an act of Love and Mercy from Jesus.

- Our sins will be shown to us and this will make us feel tremendous sorrow and shame when they are revealed to us. Others will be so sickened and shocked by the way in which their sins will be revealed that they will drop dead before they have a chance to ask for forgiveness.

- Everyone will see the state of their soul before God – the good they have done in their lives, the grief they have inflicted on others and all that which they failed to do.

- Many people will fall down and cry tears of relief. Tears of joy and happiness. Tears of wonder and love.

- For, at last, it will be possible to live a new life thereafter when we know the full truth.

- Jesus is now asking everyone to pray for those souls who will die of shock who may be in mortal sin. Everyone needs to prepare now. Jesus asks that all ask for the forgiveness of their sins in advance of The Warning.

Proverbs has much to say about God's wisdom and our discernment. Chapter 4, verse 23 tells us to be careful how we think, as our lives are shaped by our thoughts. "People who listen when they are corrected will live, but those who will not admit that they are wrong are in danger" (Prov. 10:17). Scripture says that we have all gone astray, each following the desires of our own heart and ways (Isa. 53:6). But the Lord is giving us a chance to return to Him now because a man's days are numbered according to Job 14:5. So think about it---What if? And ask yourself, am I ready?

***

FOR MORE INFORMATION ON:
"The Book of Truth"
www.TheWarningSecondComing.com

CONCLUSION

I occasionally ask myself; "What is an ordinary person like me who has no authority as a theologian trying to say?" My goal is to tell a story of my faith journey, never to preach or convince anyone, yet I believe that my experience was for a purpose. If you are a believer in any way, you must not discount any words of wisdom, particularly if they are backed by the Word of God. Pray for discernment, take what is good, and leave what is misleading: "Put all things to the test: keep what is good and avoid every kind of evil" (1 Thess. 5:20-22).

God, Take Over; I Am Finished is a book about coming to terms with the truth of our dependency on God alone, not man or self. It is a cry for mercy after realizing that if God doesn't help you, it's over. I discovered the power of God's strength made manifest in my weakness, and His love in suffering as I allowed Him to take control with a simple attitude of "Lord; Thy Will Be Done." Only then did I begin to see a gain in the pain as its written: "My son, do not despise the LORD's discipline, and do not resent his rebuke because the Lord disciplines those he loves, as a father the son he delights in" (Prov. 3:11-12).

The Lord allowed me to live through the valley experience and emerge victorious to write about it; for encouragement and building up, and, to testify to the glory of God that sunshine comes after the rain. Now, when I minister to someone who is hurting or going through similar experiences, it would not just be my words for I know what it's like. I have been there and can understand what the person is going through. My hope and prayer is that the testimonies, advice, and divine revelation shared in this book will bring encouragement, strength, endurance, and perseverance to every heart and to trust God more in all circumstances.

Our call to eternal life brings peace and comfort in the hearts of those who believe and hope for it, achieve through conversion and repentance. It does not matter, who you are, where you have been and the path you found yourself now, God is a Restorer and, ever ready to forgive all things at all times. Bring It On, He will make you anew again. Scripture says that He forgives us not because of who we are, but for who He is: "I, even, I am the one who wipes out your transgressions for My own sake, And I will not remember your sins" (Isa. 43:25).

It is clear that we need heavenly grace to please God. By our own will alone, none of us can please Him. You can accomplish your desires and goals, as well as attain spiritual height and growth through prayer and union with divine will of God. As I wrote this book, I constantly prayed to the Holy Spirit to release an anointing so that those willing to submit to God would be empowered to love perfectly, pray better, forgive faster, live happier, and surrender to His leading. I pray for the restoration of marriages and finances, for the renewal and healing of the mind, body, and soul. I pray for peace in your heart, in your family, and in your world.

I have opened up my heart and revealed the pain, and now I testify about my restoration that God may be glorified. The Holy Spirit healed every wound and gradually unites my desires to entwine with His will for me. I pray that He who has begun a good work in us will bring it to completion, in the name of Jesus, Amen (Phil. 1:6).

The next chapter concludes with a powerful call of conversion; a message from our Savior and Lord Jesus Christ to every single person; including those followers who could use His amazing grace to press-on. Your ability to excel and be victorious depends on your complete cooperation with God's plans for you.

Finally, decide now, for good and for God, that through obedience you will receive your reward. If after minutes, hours, days, weeks, months, or years of reading this book, you feel it has made a difference in your life, please write me with your testimony so that other people may be encouraged and believe that the Word of God never fails.

You may follow me online on Facebook & Twitter @ GodTakeOver. Visit me at www.cathyagada.com to leave your testimony and comments. Email cathy@ctkpublishing.net for speaking engagement.

Many thanks for reading and God bless.

THE CALL TO CONVERSION

*On Sunday, November 21st, 2010 Jesus Call all mankind to conversion[xxi] –
As, has just been said: "If Today you hear his voice, do not harden your hearts as
you did in the rebellion" (Hebrews 3:15). It is a message of hope and a way for
believers to move forward victoriously. Listen to the call:*

"Today, I bring a Message of hope and peace to all of My
children who may feel that these Messages have represented fear.
Know that, for even those of you who find it difficult to believe in
Me, My Eternal Father and the Holy Spirit, you must not worry. Many
of you, My dear children, want to believe, but because of your
reasoning and logic, where you evaluate all things based on rational
thinking, you will find it hard to believe in the supernatural.

Fear not. By praying, even just once a day and asking My
Sacred Heart to pour out My Love on you, you will very soon feel
differently. Many of you – those who are vague in your beliefs – envy
others with a deep faith. You must understand that I love all of you.
Like a parent, each of you holds a deep and special place in My Heart.
You must never feel you are not worthy of My Love.

Did I not love you to such an extent that I willingly gave up
My life for you, in the hope that you would be given a second chance
to come back to Me?

Children, you will always be pushed aside by others for

expressing a belief in your Divine Creator. When this happens remember that this is something that man must suffer on this Earth, for their love for Me. Never let this belief in Me, your Divine Savior, fade or be hidden from those who will look at you with pity.

Yes, many of My children, influenced by human reasoning and logic, deliberately placed in their closed souls, will question your beliefs. To insult you further they will be embarrassed by your faith, and while they will not publicly admit it, they feel a curious jealousy. This jealousy springs from the certainty that dawn on them that inside their souls there is emptiness. No matter how hard they look inward they cannot understand why this is the case. Meanwhile, you, the believer, will undergo humiliation through the embarrassed eyes of onlookers with a weak faith or none at all.

Never be afraid or embarrassed to own up to the love you have in your hearts for My Eternal Father. Be open about your faith. Wear your love proudly, for Me, for all to see. By doing so you are leading by example.

Never try too hard to impose, through logical reasoning, your beliefs to non-believers, in an aggressive manner. Instead show your brothers and sisters, love and support, even though you know they need guidance. When they see the forthright manner, in which you voice your love for Me openly and with joy in your heart, they will begin to wonder.

By leading others, through the example of love, respect and good deeds, they will be drawn towards the Light. Many won't understand why, at first. But in time, and especially by the power of your prayers, they will walk towards Me.

I urge you all to pray for the conversion of all souls. This includes those people known to you, personally, whom you feel are in need of prayers, for difficulties they encounter in this life. Pray too for the conversion of those poor children lost to Me through the darkness, which blinds them to the Truth. Pray especially with compassion and love for those who follow, actively, the path of the deceiver. They, more than anyone else, need your prayers.

Make known, to all you come in contact with, details, as to how each of them can be redeemed, even at the moment of death, by reciting the Chaplet of the **Divine Mercy**[xxii].

Please, please give this to everyone who will listen. Urge them, if you dare, to read it and remember, because if you do and they do recite it in their last few breaths, they can and will be saved by Me. Never be ashamed of the Crosses you wear. Never feel insulted when non-believers laugh or poke fun at you when you pray. Never be ashamed of the Crosses you wear for protection. Do not hide these symbols of the love you hold for Me, your Divine Savior, My Eternal Father or the Holy Spirit. By proudly wearing these badges of holy honor, you will lead others towards Me. Despite outward scorn you may experience from these people, inwardly, they envy you for your faith.

Many of these observers feel a hollow emptiness inside, due to their lack of faith. Prayer, My children, can help Me win over their souls. Say this pray for them.

"My dear Lord, I hold out my arms to ask You to take my beloved brother/sister into Your tender Arms. Bless them with Your Sacred Blood and give them the grace needed to allow them to receive the Spirit of Your Love, to lead them into eternal salvation."

When you, My believers, are openly challenged by others about your faith, first say this:

"I am a follower of Christ, Who suffered death at the hands of non-believers. Because of that, as a follower of Christ, I will always suffer indignity, because of

my love for Him, from others. That is the Cross I bear and am proud of this fact. He, my Savior, died, not just for my sins, but for yours."

When they proudly boast of the fact they are agnostic or atheists tell them this. Ask them if they will feel different when their life on this Earth draws to a close? Then give them this advice. On your deathbed remember this prayer of the **Divine Mercy** (refer to page 122 for how to pray Divine Mercy chaplet) even if you are still unsure. Open your hearts and ask My Eternal Father to forgive them. Remember My promise. As Judge, as well as your Savior, I will forgive – right up to each of My children's last breath on this Earth. Tell them to pray hard, so that they can open their hearts just once.

Prayer leads all My children closer to My Kingdom on Earth when Heaven and Earth will merge as one. The power of prayer will only be truly understood when My children open their hearts and call out. Ask, and if it is God's Will, your prayers will be answered.

Never deny your children the Sacrament of Baptism

Lastly, pray for the little children, your sons and daughters and the youth in the world. Each of them deserves to be shown the Truth. They were not shown the Truth of God's Love or given guidance by their parents, due to the spiritual darkness, which has existed on Earth over the last two decades. Even if your own faith is weak, do not shirk your duty, as parents, to give them access to the Sacraments, especially Baptism.

Never take it upon yourself to deny this most important Sacrament to your own child. Many parents, who proudly stand firm, as they shout about their views of disbelief, are damaging their children's souls. Give your children the gift of the Sacraments. In time, they will either thank you for this or deny Me. That will be up to them. Deny Me if you must, but do not steal the souls of My children. You may be their parents on Earth, but they are the children of My

Eternal Father, the Creator and Maker of all things. Do not try to take them into the darkness with you. Remember again, that despite your own beliefs, I love you all."

Your Divine Savior and Judge

Jesus Christ, Son of the Eternal Father

PRAYERS

Jesus, I trust in You

My God, I love You

Jesus Son of God, have mercy on me a sinner

SEAL OF THE TRINITY GOD

This special prayer is a Gift from God the Father given to prophet Maria Divine Mercy for the protection of all God's Children (received February 20, 2012). All who accept this Seal will be offered protection for each and every one of you and your families during the period in the lead up to the Second Coming of Christ.

Rise now and accept My Seal, the Seal of the Living God. Recite this Crusade Prayer to acknowledge My Seal and accept it with love, joy and gratitude.

O My God, My Loving Father, I accept with love and gratitude Your Divine Seal of Protection. Your Divinity encompasses my body and soul for eternity. I bow in humble thanksgiving and offer my deep love and loyalty to You my Beloved Father. I beg You to protect me and my loved ones with this special Seal and I pledge my life to Your service forever and ever. I love You Dear Father. I console You in these times Dear Father. I offer You the Body, Blood, Soul and Divinity of Your dearly beloved Son In atonement for the sins of the world and for the salvation of all Your children. Amen.

Go, My children and do not fear. Trust in Me, Your beloved Father, who lovingly created each of you. I know every single soul, every part of you is known to Me. Not one of you is loved less than the other. Because of this I do not want to lose one soul. Not one.

Please continue to pray My Divine Mercy Chaplet every day. One day, you will understand why this purification is needed.

Your Loving Father In Heaven
God the Most High

HOW TO RECITE THE DIVINE MERCY CHAPLET:

This prayer was given by our Lord Jesus Christ to St. Faustina as referenced on page [114, 115]. He urges all mankind to say this prayer; for even on the dying bed, His mercy would envelop anyone who invokes His mercy by it.

1. Make the Sign of the Cross

Optional Opening Prayers
"You expired, Jesus, but the source of life gushed forth for souls, and the ocean of mercy opened up for the whole world. O Fount of Life, unfathomable Divine Mercy, envelops the whole world and empty Yourself out upon us.

O Blood and Water, which gushed forth from the Heart of Jesus as a fountain of Mercy for us, I trust in You!"

The Chaplet of Divine Mercy is recited using ordinary Rosary Beads of five decades.

2. On the Five large Beads of Each Decade Say:
"Eternal Father, I offer you the Body and Blood, Soul and Divinity of Your Dearly Beloved Son, Our Lord, Jesus Christ, in atonement for our sins and those of the whole world".

3. On the Ten Small Beads of Each Decade Say Ten Times:
"For the sake of His sorrowful Passion, have mercy on us and on the whole world".
(Repeat for the remaining 5 decades)

4 Conclude with Holy God saying:
"Holy God, Holy Mighty One, Holy Immortal One, have mercy on us and on the whole world." (Repeat three times)

Optional Closing Prayer"
Eternal God, in whom mercy is endless and the treasury of compassion — inexhaustible, look kindly upon us and increase Your mercy in us, that in difficult moments we might not despair nor become despondent, but with great confidence submit ourselves to Your holy will, which is Love and Mercy itself. Amen!

CRUSADE PRAYERS

Please pray the Jesus-To-Mankind crusade prayers given to and for all mankind. These prayers bring repentance and conversion to non-believers, luke-worm and hardened souls, and will help mitigate the coming persecutions and chastisement as prophesied in the book of "Revelation" before the second coming. Jesus asks that we form prayer groups, and pray together with family, friends, or church members. Pray it for you, your loved ones and for anyone you want to be saved

Pray without ceasing and when in doubt ask the Holy Spirit for discernment. . JTM Crusade prayer warriors are among the numerous end-time warriors of Christ who through their selfless prayers would help save mankind. Its wisdom will bring you to a place of spiritual maturity and accelerate your personal growth.

+++

Prayer to be able to see that these messages are of Divine Origin
Jesus if this is really you please flood my soul with the sign of your love so that I can recognize you for who you are. Do not let me be deceived by lies. Show me instead your mercy by opening my eyes to the truth and the path to your new Paradise on earth.

Prayer that Jesus may reveal His presence to you
Jesus I feel lost. Open my heart to accept your love and show me the truth so that I may be saved.

Prayer for encouragement
Fill me now Oh Lord with the gift of the Holy Spirit to carry your most Holy Word to sinners who I must help save in your name. Help me to cover them, through my prayers, with your precious blood so that they

can be drawn to your Sacred Heart. Give me the gift of the Holy Spirit
so that these poor souls can revel in your New Paradise.

Prayer for each day
O my precious Jesus embrace me in your arms and allow my head
to rest upon your shoulders so that you can raise me up to your glorious
Kingdom when the time is right. Allow your precious blood to flow
over my heart that we can be united as one.

Prayer to let go of your fears
Jesus I hand you over all my concerns in this matter in confidence so that
the problem is now yours to resolve according to your most Holy Will

The Poor and Ashamed soul's Prayer
[Walk towards Me and ask Me to help... Come. Bow your heads. Push
your shame aside and ask Me to forgive you now.]

Prayer for the blind souls who are lost
God, the Most High, I come before your throne this week to plead
for the souls of My brothers and sisters who refuse to acknowledge
your existence. I urge you to fill them with your graces so that they will
open their hearts to listen to your most Holy Word

Prayer to enter Heaven
O my precious Jesus embrace me in your arms and allow my head to
 rest upon your shoulders so that you can raise me up to your glorious
Kingdom when the time is right. Allow your precious blood to flow over
 my heart that we can be united as one.

Prayer to withstand the abomination which is on the way
O My beloved Jesus I invoke your protection and ask for your mercy to
save my brothers and sisters within your church from falling victim to the
Anti-Christ. Give me the graces and protect me with your armor of
strength to stand up to the evil acts which may be perpetrated in your
Holy Name. I beg for your mercy and pledge My allegiance to your Holy
name at all times.

Prayer for the gift of enlightenment
O Jesus cover me with your precious blood and fill me with the Holy Spirit
so that I can discern whether these words come from you. Humble me in
spirit. Receive my pleas with mercy and open my heart to the truth.

Prayer plea from God the Father
God the Most High, in the Name of Your beloved Son Jesus Christ,
Whom You sacrificed to save us, Your poor children, from the fires
of Hell, hear our prayer. May we offer our humble sacrifices and accept
trials and tribulations as a means to gain the salvation of all souls during
The Warning. We plead with You to forgive sinners who find it hard to

turn back and accept Your Merciful Goodness to make the necessary sacrifices as You see fit to redeem them in Your Holy Eyes.

Prayer to mitigate the circumstances of persecution, which is being perpetrated behind closed doors. God the Father, in the Name of Your beloved Son Jesus Christ I beg of You to stop this abomination to control Your children. Please protect all Your children in these terrible times so that we may find peace and dignity to live our lives free from the Evil One.

Prayer to never give up when you feel down
Jesus if you can hear me Then listen to my call for help
Please help me deal with those who cause me pain
Help me to stop envy taking over my life and to stop me wishing for
things I cannot have. Instead open my heart to you dear Jesus
Help me to feel real love – your love And to feel true peace in my heart.
Amen

Prayer to become little
Heavenly Father help me to become little, as a child, in your eyes.
I ask for your graces to fall upon me so I can respond to your call
to save all of your children. Amen.

Prayer for the graces of wisdom, calm and discernment
O Jesus help me to see the truth of your Holy Word at all times and
remain loyal to your teachings no matter how much I am forced to reject
you.

Prayer for the Key to the New Paradise
Dear Father, it is I, Your lost child, who, so confused and blind, that
without Your Help, Your Love, I am nothing. Save me through the Love of
Your Son, Jesus Christ, and give me the Key to Your New Paradise on
Earth. Amen.

Prayer for Salvation
O my Lord lead me to your kingdom and protect me from the darkness
that has engulfed my soul. Hear me now O Sacred Heart and through
your goodness let your light of love and protection shine through.

Atheist's Prayer
God if you are the truth reveal to me the sign of your love. Open my heart
to receive guidance. If you exist let me feel your love so I can see the
truth. Pray for me now

Prayer for non-believers who laugh, poke fun at or outwardly scorn those who pray
My dear lord I hold out my arms to ask you to take my beloved

brother/sister into your tender arms. Bless them with your sacred blood and give them the grace needed to allow them receive the spirit of your love to lead them into eternal salvation.

Prayer to sustain faith and belief in God's Message for the world
Dearest Jesus, when I am down, lift me up.
When I doubt, enlighten me.
When I am in sorrow, show me Your Love.
When I criticize, help me to remain silent.
When I judge another in public, seal my lips.
When I utter blasphemies, in Your Name, redeem me and bring me back into Your protection.
When I lack courage, give me the sword I need to do battle and save the souls You desire.
When I resist Your Love help me to surrender and abandon myself, completely, within Your Loving care.
When I wander away, help me to find the Path of Truth.
When I question Your Word, give me the answers I seek.
Help me to be patient, loving and kind, even to those who curse You.
Help me to forgive those who offend me and give me the grace I need to follow You to the ends of the earth. Amen

+++

If you want to know more about Jesus-To-Mankind crusade prayer groups, visit: http://crusadeprayergroup.org/crusade.html or follow the messages at http://thewarningsecondcoming.com/messages.

NOTES & REFERENCES

[i] Maria Divine Mercy, *The Book of Truth*, Vols. 1-2 (Coma Books, 2012).

[ii] Message, "All Mankind Will Have Free Will until Their Will Unites with the Divine Will of the Father," April 25, 2011, ww.thewarningsecondcoming.com.

[iii] The Blessed Sacrament of Eucharistic Adoration is the exposition of the Body and Blood of Christ in the form of the consecrated Host; Catholics believe in the true presence of Jesus Christ in the form of the Host consecrated by a Catholic priest. It is a place of holiness where perpetual adoration is accorded to our Lord, and where miracles of the heart and conversions occur.

[iv] *Praise the Lord*, The Christian Television Network (TBN), 2012.

[v] Message, "Love Is the Way to Salvation," February 5, 2011.

[vi] Message, "How to Ask Me to Help You Resolve Your Worries," August 17, 2011.

[vii] Message, "Jesus Calls to Children All Over the World," January 8, 2012.

[viii] Healing Service Seminar Talk by Fr. Bramlage - Divine Mercy Sunday Retreat, Mesquite TX, 2013.

[ix] Newsmax Health, https://www.newsmaxstore.com/newsletters/mhr/prayer_text_order.cfm

[x] Message, "Please Take This New Gift of Healing I Present to You Now," January 15, 2013.

[xi] Message, "Come to Me All of You Who Feel Unworthy. I Am Waiting for You," June 21, 2012.

[xii] Message, "Stairway to Spiritual Perfection," November 24, 2010.

[xiii] Message, "Call on Believers to Convert Souls," November 26th, 2010

xiv Message, "Quest for Wealth," November 30th, 2010

xv Catherine Aniebonam, *Making It Work: Inspirations for Christian Marriage and Life* (2006).

xvi Message, "Hatred Is the Cause of All Evil in the World and It Takes Many Forms," August 26, 2012.

xvii The Isaiah Ministry — a prayer and Bible study group.

xviii Message and talk given by a visionary, Ivan Dragicevic, in Medjugorje where the Blessed Mother's appearance has been reported (Medjugorje, 2002)

xix Message – "I call on all of you who don't know Me", April 30th, 2012,

xx Message: "Love is More Powerful than Hatred", March 14, 2012

xxi Jesus Message to MDM - On Sunday, November 21st, 2010 titled: "Conversion" -thewarningsecondcoming.com

xxii Chaplet of Divine Mercy Prayer – given to St. Fustian (1935). The Lord requested that this Chaplet be said not only by Sr. Faustina, but all mankind.

www.ingramcontent.com/pod-product-compliance
Lightning Source LLC
LaVergne TN
LVHW011243080426
835509LV00005B/607